Melion

A Medieval Werewolf Tale with Original Text, Translations, and Word Lists

Translated by Matthew Leigh Embleton

Copyright ©2025 Matthew Leigh Embleton. All rights reserved.

Melion

Melion..4
Word List *(Old French to English)*...32
Word List *(English to Old French)*...47

Cover: Old French text over an outline of France. Author's design.

The original Old French text is in the public domain.
This translation ©2021 Matthew Leigh Embleton
©2025 Matthew Leigh Embleton (This Edition)

Acknowledgments

I have long been fascinated by languages and history, and I am very grateful to the special people in my life who have supported and encouraged me in my work. Thank you for believing in me. You know who you are.

Introduction

The author of Melion is unknown, but it is believed to have been written sometime between 1190 and 1204. It is one of around 10 anonymous 'lais' of that time drawing upon Breton and Arthurian myths and legends. These myths and legends often contained elements of the supernatural to ornament what were moral tales of heroism and chivalry.

It is written in the Picard dialect of Old French, part of the 'Langues d'oïl' dialect continuum of Gallo-Romance languages. Old French is the result of a gradual separation from Vulgar Latin and Common Romance, coming into contact with influences from Gaulish (Continental Celtic), and Frankish (Germanic).

The text is presented in the original Old French, with a literal word-for-word line-by-line translation, and a Modern English translation, all side-by-side. In this way, it is possible to see and feel how Old French worked and how it has evolved.

Also included is a word list with 1,012 Old French words translated in to English, and 946 English words translated into Old French.

This book is designed to be of use and interest to anyone with a passion for the Old French language, French history, or languages and history in general.

Melion

	Old French	Literal	English
1	Al tans que rois Artus regnoit -	At time when king Arthur ruled	At the time when King Arthur reigned
2	Cil ki les terres conqueroit,	He who the lands conquered,	He who conquered lands
3	Et qui dona les riches dons	And who gave the rich gifts	And who gave rich gifts
4	As chevaliers et as barons -	The knights and the barons	To knights and to barons
5	Avoit od lui .I. bacheler;	Had with him one knight;	He had with him a knight;
6	Melïon l'ai oï nomer.	Melion I have heard called.	I have heard him called Melion.
7	Molt par estoit cortois et prous	Very by was courtly and noble	He was very courtly and noble,
8	Et amer se faisoit a tos.	And loved he was-made by all.	And he made himself beloved by all.
9	Molt ert de grant chevalerie	Many was of great knights	He was in a great band of knights
10	Et de cortoise compaignie.	And of courtly company.	And of courtly company.
11	Li rois ot molt riche maisnie;	The king had very rich household;	The king kept a very rich household;
12	Par tot le mont estoit proisie	By all the world was praised	It was praised by all the world
13	De cortoisie et de proece	Of courtesy and of prowess	For its courtesy and prowess
14	Et de bonté et de largece.	And of excellence and of largesse.	And its excellence and generosity.
15	A icel jor lor veu faisoient,	And one day their vows they-were-making,	One day they were making their vows
16	Et sachiés bien k'il le gardoient.	And be-sure well that they kept.	And you may be very sure that they kept them.
17	Cil Melïons .I. en voa	This Melion one of vow	This Melion made one vow
18	Que a grant mal li atorna:	Which to great harm to-him returned:	Which returned on him great harm:
19	Il dist ja n'ameroit pucele,	He said never enamoured maiden,	He said he would never love a maiden,
20	Que tant seroit gentil ne bele,	Who so-much was noble or beautiful,	No matter how noble or beautiful,
21	Que nul autre home eüst amé,	Who any other man would-have loved,	Who had loved any other man

Melion

	Old French	Literal	English
22	*Ne que de nul eüst parlé.*	Or who of any would-have spoken.	Or even had spoken of any.
23	*Une grant piece fu ensi:*	A great time happened so-as-this:	For a great time matters stood like this:
24	*Cil ki le veu orent oï*	They who this vow prayed heard	Those who had heard this vow
25	*En pluisors lieus le recorderent*	Then many places this repeated	Repeated it in many places
26	*Et as puceles le conterent;*	And the maidens they heard;	And the maidens they heard;
27	*Et qant les puceles l'oïrent*	And when the maidens heard	And when the maidens heard
28	*Molt durement l'en enhaïrent.*	Much greatly him they-hated.	They hated him for it very much.
29	*Celes ki es canbres estoient*	Those who in-those chambers they-were	Those who were ladies-in-waiting
30	*Et ki la roïne servoient,*	And who the queen they-served,	And who served the queen,
31	*Dont il en i ot plus de cent,*	Of-whom they of there had more than a-hundred,	Of whom there were more than a hundred,
32	*En ont tenu .I. parlement:*	On-which they beheld a meeting:	Held a meeting about it:
33	*Dïent jamais ne l'ameront,*	They-said never not him-they-would-love,	They said they would never love him
34	*N'encontre lui ne parleront;*	nor-meet him not they-speak;	Nor speak to him;
35	*Dame nel voloit regarder,*	Lady nor wished-to look-at-him,	No lady wished to look at him,
36	*Ne pucelë a lui parler.*	Nor maiden to him speak.	Nor any maiden to speak to him.
37	*Qant Melïon ice oï,*	When Melion this heard,	When Melion heard this,
38	*Molt durement s'en asopli;*	Very hard was-he downcast;	He was very downcast;
39	*Ne voloit mais querre aventure,*	Not he-wished more to-seek adventure,	He no longer wished to seek adventure
40	*Ne d'armes porter n'avoit cure.*	Nor of-arms to-bear not-having a-care.	Nor did he care to bear arms.
41	*Molt fu dolans, molt asopli,*	Much became sorrow, much downcast,	He was sorrowful, very unhappy,
42	*Et de son pris alques perdi.*	And of his esteem somewhat lost.	And he lost his esteem somewhat.
43	*Li rois le sot, molt l'en pesa,*	This the-king he found-out, much him weighed-upon,	The king found this out, it weighed very heavily on him;

Melion

	Old French	Literal	English
44	Mander le fist, a lui parla.	Commanded he be, to him to-speak.	He had Melion sent for and spoke
45	'Melïons', fait li rois Artus,	Melion', said he king Arthur,	Melion', said King Arthur,
46	'Tes grans sens qu'est il devenus,	'Your great sense what has become,	What has become of your great sense,
47	Ton pris et ta chevalerie?	Your esteem and your chivalry?	Your esteem and your chivalry?
48	Di que tu as, nel celes mie.	Say what you have, nor hide none-at-all.	Say what's wrong, hide none of it.
49	Se tu veus terre ne manoir,	If you want land or a-manor,	If you want land or a manor,
50	N'autre cose que puisse avoir,	or-other things which I-may have,	Or any other thing I may have,
51	Se il est en ma roiauté,	If it is in my realm,	If it is in my realm
52	Tu l'avras a ta volenté.	You shall-have as your wish.	You shall have it as you wish.
53	Volentiers te rehaiteroie',	Willingly you comfort,	I would willingly comfort you',
54	Ce dist li rois, 'se jo pooie.	This said the king, 'if I could.	Said the king, 'if I could.
55	Un castel ai sor cele mer;	A castle have on the sea;	I have a castle on the coast;
56	En tot cest siecle n'a itel.	In all this age not-has-been the-same.	There's not such a one in this age.
57	Beax est de bois et de riviere	Beautiful it-is of forests and of rivers	It has beautiful woods, rivers
58	Et de forest que molt as chiere.	And of forest that much you dearly-love.	And forests, that you love so much.
59	Cel te donrai por rehaitier,	This you i-will-give for comfort,	I shall give you this to comfort you;
60	Bien t'i porras esbanoier.'	Well you may enjoy'.	You can enjoy yourself there very well'.
61	Li rois li a en fief doné;	The king him to of-it fief gave;	The king gave it to him in fief;
62	Melïons l'en a mercïé.	Melion him he thanked.	Melion thanked him for it.
63	A son castel en est alé,	To his castle on is going,	He set out for his castle,
64	.C. chevaliers i a mené.	A-hundred knights with he took.	And took a hundred knights there.
65	Li païs bien li conteça	He the-country well him contented	The country pleased him well,

Melion

	Old French	Literal	English
66	*Et la forest que molt ama.*	And the forest which much he-loved.	And the forest, which he loved very much.
67	*Qant il i ot .I. an esté,*	When he there away one year had-been,	When he had been there for a year,
68	*Molt a le païs enamé,*	Much of the country he-loved,	He loved the country greatly,
69	*Car ja deduit ne demandast*	For already pleasure not asked-for	For there was no pleasure he may ask for
70	*Que en la forest ne trovast.*	Which in the forest could-not find.	That he could not find in the forest.
71	*Un jor estoit alé chacier*	One day was going the-hunt	One day Melion went hunting,
72	*Melïon et si forestier.*	Melion and his foresters.	Melion and his foresters.
73	*Od lui furent si veneor,*	Among him had his huntsmen,	Among him had his huntsmen,
74	*Ki l'amerent de bone amor*	Who him-loved of good love	Who loved him truly
75	*Car ce estoit lor liges sire;*	Because he was their liege sire;	Because he was their liege sire;
76	*Totes honors en lui remire.*	All honour was him admired.	All honour was reflected in him.
77	*Tost orent .I. grant cerf trové,*	Quickly had one great stag found,	Soon they found a great stag;
78	*Tost l'orent pris et descoplé.*	Immediately had took and unleashed.	Quickly they took and unleashed the hounds.
79	*En une lande s'aresta*	And one land he-stopped	Melion stopped in a heath
80	*Por sa meute k'il escouta.*	For how might which-he listen.	So he could listen for the pack of hounds.
81	*Od lui estoit uns escuiers,*	Among, with him, him was one squire,	With him was a squire;
82	*En sa main tenoit .II. levriers.*	And his hand held two greyhounds.	He was restraining two greyhounds in his hand.
83	*En la lande, qu'est verde et bele,*	In his heath, which-is green and beautiful,	In this heath, which was green and beautiful,
84	*Vit Melïons une pucele*	Saw Melion a maiden	Melion saw a maiden
85	*Venir sor .I. bel palefroi;*	Coming on one beautiful palfrey;	Approaching on a handsome palfrey;
86	*Molt erent riche si conroi.*	Much were rich of the-trappings.	The trappings were most rich.
87	*Un vermeil samit ot vestu,*	A vermillion rich-silk had wearing,	She was dressed in vermillion silk

Melion

	Old French	Literal	English
88	*Estoit a las molt bien cosu;*	Was of lace very well sewn;	Which was sewn well with laces;
89	*A son col .I. mantel d'ermine;*	On her shoulders one mantle of-ermine;	Around her shoulders was an ermine
90	*Ainc meillor n'afubla roïne.*	Rather better than-worn a-queen.	No queen ever wore better.
91	*Gent cors et bele espauleüre,*	Beautiful body and elegant shoulders,	A pleasing figure, elegant shoulders
92	*Et blonde la cheveleüre.*	And blonde her hair.	And blonde was her hair.
93	*Petite bouche bien mollee*	Petite mouth well shaped	A nicely shaped petite mouth,
94	*Et comme rose encoloree;*	And as rose coloured;	The colour of a rose;
95	*Les ex ot vairs, clers et rians:*	Her eyes with bright, clear and sparlking:	She had bright eyes, clear and sparkling:
96	*Molt estoit bele en tos samblans.*	Much was beauty in all appearance.	She was very beautiful in her whole appearance.
97	*Seule venoit sans compaignie,*	Alone came without company,	She came alone without company,
98	*Molt par fu gente et escavie.*	Much by was elegant and charming.	And was most elegant and charming.
99	*Melïon contre lui en va;*	Melion to-greet her he went;	Melion went to meet her;
100	*Molt belement le salua.*	Very politely he greeted.	He greeted her very politely.
101	*'Bele', dist il, 'jo vos salu*	'Fair-lady', said he, 'I you greet	Fair lady', he said, 'I greet you
102	*Del glorious, le roi Jesu.*	From glorious, the king Jesus.	From glorious, the king Jesus.
103	*Dites moi dont vos estes nee*	Tell me of-where you are born	Tell me where you were born
104	*Et que ici vos a menee.'*	And what here you has brought'.	And what has brought you here'.
105	*Cele respont: 'Jel vos dirai,*	This responded: 'I-will you tell,	She replied: 'I shall tell you about it,
106	*Que ja de mot n'en mentirai.*	For I of words not-of shall-lie.	I shall not tell you a word of a lie.
107	*Je sui assez de haut parage*	I am rather of high family	I am of very high birth
108	*Et nee de gentil lignage.*	And born of noble lineage.	And born of noble lineage.
109	*D'Yrlande sui a vos venue;*	From-Ireland I-am to you arriving;	I have come to you from Ireland;

Melion

	Old French	Literal	English
110	Sachiés que je sui molt vo drue.	Know-you that I am very-much your mistress.	Know that I am entirely your lover.
111	Onques home fors vos n'amai,	Never man except you have-I-loved,	I have never loved a man other than you
112	Ne jamais plus n'en amerai.	Nor never another not shall-I-love.	Nor shall I ever love another.
113	Forment vos ai oï loer,	Greatly you have-I heard praised,	I have heard you greatly praised,
114	Onques ne voloie altre amer	Never none wished other to-love	I never desired to love any other
115	Fors vos tot seul; ne jamais jor	Except you completely only; nor never a-day	But you alone; never at any time
116	Vers nul autre n'avrai amor.'	To none other shall-I love'.	Shall I have love for anyone else'.
117	Quant Melïons a antendu	When Melion this heard	When Melion realised
118	Que si veu erent atendu,	That if wishes were attended,	That his vows were fulfilled,
119	Par mi les flans l'a enbracie,	By him his arms her embraced,	He put his arms around her waist
120	Et plus de trente fois baisie.	And more-than of thirty times kissed.	And kissed her more than thirty times.
121	Puis a tote sa gent mandee,	Then had all his people sent-for,	Then he sent for all his people
122	L'aventure lor a contee.	The-adventure theirs he recounted.	And told them what had happened.
123	Cil ont veüe la pucele;	That they saw the maiden;	They looked at the maiden;
124	El roialme n'avoit tant bele.	The the-kingdom had-not as-much beauty.	There was none so beautiful in the kingdom.
125	A son castel l'en a mené,	To his castle her he took,	Melion took her to his castle;
126	Molt ont grant joie demené.	Much they great rejoicing of-took.	They took of great rejoicing.
127	A grant richoise l'espousa,	With great splendour her-he-married,	He married her with great splendor
128	Et molt grant joie en demena;	And much great joy in took;	And took great joy about it;
129	.XV. jors a li pas duré.	fifteen days had this passed endured.	The celebrations lasted fifteen days.
130	.III. ans le tint en grant chierté;	three years he held in great affection;	For three years he held her in great affection:
131	.II. fiex en ot en ces .III. ans,	two sons he had in the three years,	He had two sons by her in these three years

Melion

	Old French	Literal	English
132	Molt par en fu lies et joians.	Much by he became glad and joyful.	And was very glad and joyful about it.
133	Un jor en la forest ala;	One day in the forest he-went;	One day he went into the forest;
134	Sa chiere feme ot lui mena.	His dear wife had he taken.	He took his dear wife with him.
135	Un cerf trova, si l'ont chacié,	A stag found, and this-they chased,	He found a stag, and they chased it
136	Et il s'en fuit, le col baissié.	And it then fled, his neck lowered.	And it fled, its neck lowered.
137	.I. escuier o lui avoit	A squire with him he-had	He had a squire with him
138	Ki son bercerië portoit.	Who his quiver carried.	Who was carrying his quiver.
139	En une lande sont entré.	And a heath they entered.	They went on to a heath.
140	En .I. buisson a regardé;	And one bush he looked-upon;	Melion looked into a bush:
141	Un molt grant cerf i voit estant.	One very great stag he saw standing.	He saw a great stag standing there.
142	Sa feme regarde en riant.	His wife he-looked and laughed.	Laughing, Melion looked at his wife.
143	'Dame', fait il, 'se jo voloie,	'Lady', said he, 'if you wish,	'Lady', he said, 'if you wish,
144	.I. molt grant cerf vos mosterroie:	A very large stag you I-will-show:	I would show you a great stag:
145	Veés le la en cel buisson.'	See it there in that bush'.	See it there in that bush'.
146	'Par foi!' fait ele, 'Melïon,	'By faith said she, 'Melion,	'By my faith', she said, 'Melion,
147	Sachiés se jo de cel cerf n'ai	Know-you if I of that stag do-not-have	Know that if I do not have some of that stag
148	Que jo jamais ne mangerai.'	Then I never shall-not i-will-eat'.	I shall never eat again'.
149	Del palefroi chaï pasmee,	From palfrey fell fainting,	She fell from her palfrey, fainting,
150	Et Melïons l'a relevee.	And Melion her picked-up.	And Melion picked her up.
151	Qant ne le pot reconforter,	When not he could comfort,	When he could not comfort her,
152	Molt durement prist a plorer.	Very sorely took to weeping.	She began to weep bitterly.
153	'Dame', dist il, 'por Deu merci,	'Lady', said he, 'for God's mercy,	'Lady', he said, 'for the grace of God,

Melion

	Old French	Literal	English
154	*Ne plorés mais, jo vos en pri.*	Not i-implore-you more, I you with pray.	Never cry, I beg of you.
155	*J'ai en ma main .I. tel anel;*	I on my hand one such ring;	I have on my hand such a ring;
156	*Ves le ci en mon doit manel.*	Se it here on my finger my-hand.	See it here on my ring-finger.
157	*.II. pieres a ens el caston:*	two stones has on its casting:	It has two stones in its casting:
158	*Onques si faites ne vit on;*	Never such work no-one saw of;	No-one has ever seen such work;
159	*L'une est blance, l'autre vermeille.*	Of-one is white, the-other crimson.	One stone is white, the other crimson.
160	*Oïr en poés grant merveille:*	Hear of may great marvel:	You may hear a great marvel of them:
161	*De la blance me toucerés*	Of the white me touch	You will touch me with the white stone
162	*Et sor mon chief le meterés*	And on my head it place	And place it on my head
163	*Qant jo serai despoilliés nus,*	When I will-be unclothed nude,	When I am undressed and nude,
164	*Leus devenrai, grans et corsus.*	Wolf I-shall-become, great and strong.	And I shall become a great strong wolf.
165	*Por vostre amor le cerf prendrai*	For your love the stag capture	For love of you, I shall capture the stag
166	*Et del lart vos aporterai.*	And of the-article you I-shall-bring.	And bring some of its meat back to you.
167	*Por Deu vos pri, ci m'atendés*	For God to-you I-pray, here wait-for-me	I pray you, for God's sake, wait for me here
168	*Et ma despoille me gardés.*	And my clothes mine guard.	And guard my clothing.
169	*Je vos lais ma vie et ma mort:*	I you leave my life and my death:	I leave you my life and my death:
170	*Il n'i auroit nul reconfort*	There never have none recovery	There will be no recovery
171	*Se de l'autre touciés n'estoie;*	If of the-other touched I-shall-not-be;	If I am not touched with the other stone;
172	*Jamais nul jor hom ne seroie.'*	Never not day a-man nor become'.	I should never again be a man'.
173	*Il apela son escuier,*	He called his squire,	He called his squire,
174	*Si le commande a deschaucier.*	Him he commanded to remove-boots.	And commanded him to remove his boots.
175	*Cil vint avant, sel descaucha,*	He came forward, him removed-boots,	He came forward, removed the boots

Melion

	Old French	Literal	English
176	Et Melïon el bois entra.	And Melion in the-forest entered.	And Melion went into the woods.
177	Ses dras osta, nus est remez,	His clothes removed, nude, he remained,	He removed his clothes, remained nude,
178	De son mantel s'est afublez.	Of his cloak he-is wrapped.	And wrapped himself in his cloak.
179	Cele l'a de l'anel touchié	This she of the-ring touched	She touched him with the ring
180	Qant le vit nu et despoillié.	When she saw nude and unclothed.	When she saw him nude and undressed.
181	Lors devint leu grant et corsus:	Then became wolf great and strong:	Then he became a great and strong wolf:
182	En grant paine s'est enbatus.	In great suffering he-is entangled.	He had got himself into deep trouble.
183	Li leus s'en vait, molt tost corant	The wolf then went, very quickly running	The wolf set out, running quickly
184	La ou il vit le cerf gisant;	There where he saw the stag lying;	To where he saw the stag lying;
185	Tost se fu en la trace mis.	Immediately he became on the trace set.	He set himself to the scent at once.
186	Anchois sera grant li estris	In-choice there-will-be great his strife	There will be great strife before
187	Que il l'ait pris ne adesé,	For he has seized or approached,	He has captured or approached it
188	Ne que il avra del lardé.	Nor which he has of the-meat.	Before he has any of the meat.
189	La dame dist a l'escuier:	The lady said to the-squire:	The lady said to the squire:
190	'Or le laissons assés chacier'.	'Now him let-us very-well hunt.	'Now let him hunt for a while'.
191	Montee est, plus ne se targa,	Mounted she, more not she delayed,	She mounted, delayed no longer,
192	Et l'escuier o lui mena.	And the-squire with her took.	And took the squire with her.
193	Droit vers Yrlande, sa contree,	Directly towards Ireland, her-own country,	Straight towards Ireland, her own country,
194	En est la dame retornee.	And was the lady returned.	The lady returned.
195	Al havene vint, nef i trova;	In harbour went, ship she found;	She went to the harbour, found a ship
196	As mariniers tantost parla	The mariners immediately spoke-to	And soon spoke to the crew
197	Qui l'ont mené a Duveline,	Who they took to Dublin,	Who took her to Dublin,

Melion

	Old French	Literal	English
198	Une cité sor la marine,	A city on the sea,	A maritime city,
199	Qui son pere ert, le roi d'Yrlande;	Which her father was, the king of-Ireland;	Which belonged to her father, the King of Ireland;
200	Des or ot ce qu'ele demande.	Of-them now had that which-she asked-for.	Now she had what she required.
201	Lués qu'ele fu al port venue,	As-soon-as which-she came to the-port arrived,	As soon as she came into the port
202	A grant joie fu receüe.	With great joy was received.	She was welcomed with great joy.
203	De li lairomes aïtant,	Of her we-leave at-this-point,	We will leave her at this point,
204	De Melïon dirons avant.	Of Melion wel-tell further.	And tell further about Melion.
205	Melïon, ki le cerf chaça,	Melion, who the stag chased,	Melion, who was chasing the stag,
206	A grant merveille le hasta.	He great intensely it harried.	Harried it intently.
207	En la lande l'a conseü,	To the heath this pursued,	He pursued it on to a heath,
208	Tot maintenant l'a abatu,	All at-once this brought-down,	And at once he brought it down;
209	Puis prist de lui .I. grant lardé;	Then seized of him a great piece-of-meat;	Then he took a large piece of meat from it;
210	En sa bouche l'en a porté.	In his mouth he it carried.	He carried it away in his mouth.
211	Hastivement s'en retorna	Quickly he returned	He quickly went back
212	La ou il sa feme laissa,	There where he his wife left,	To where he had left his wife,
213	Mais il ne l'i a pas trovee;	But he not her then not found;	But he did not find her there;
214	Vers Yrlande s'en est tornee.	To Ireland was she returned.	She had set out for Ireland.
215	Molt fu dolans, ne set que face,	Very-much became sad, not knowing what to-do,	He was very sad and did not know what to do
216	Qant il ne le troeve en la place.	When he not her found in that place.	When he could not find her in that place.
217	Mais neporqant, se leus estoit,	But even-though, he wolf was,	But even though he was a wolf,
218	Sens et memoire d'ome avoit.	Sense and memory of-a-man he-had.	He retained the reason and memory of a man.
219	Tant atendi k'il avespra.	Until waited he-for evening-fell.	He waited until evening fell.

Melion

	Old French	Literal	English
220	Une nef vit que on charga,	A ship saw which being loaded,	He saw a ship being loaded
221	Ki la nuit devoit eskiper	Which that night was-to sail	Which was to sail that night
222	Et en Yrlande droit aler.	And to Ireland directly go.	And go directly to Ireland.
223	Envers cele part s'en ala,	Towards this part he-did go,	He made his way there
224	Tant atendi k'il anuita.	Until waiting for-the night-fall.	And waited until night fell.
225	Entrés i est par aventure,	Entered he this by adventure,	He took a risk and boarded it,
226	Car de sa vie n'avoit cure.	For of his live he-did-not-have care.	For he cared nothing for his life.
227	Sos une cloie s'est muciés	Under an enclosure he-is hidden	He concealed himself beneath an enclosure,
228	Et s'est tapis et enbuissiés.	And is hidden and embedded.	Crouched down and was hidden.
229	Li maronier se sont hasté,	The mariners of made haste,	The mariners made haste
230	Car molt avoient bon oré.	Because very they-had fair wind.	For they had a fair wind.
231	Lors s'en tornerent vers Yrlande;	Then they turned towards Ireland;	Then they turned towards Ireland;
232	Cascuns avoit quanque demande.	Each had what-he asked-for.	Each of them had what he wished.
233	Il sachierent amont lor voiles;	They hoisted up their sails;	They hoisted up the sails
234	Al ciel corent et as estoiles,	Of the-skies steered and the stars,	And steered by the sky and the stars,
235	Et l'endemain a l'ajornee	And the-morning of the-next-day	And the next day at dawn
236	Virent d'Yrlande la contree.	They-saw Ireland there encountered.	They saw the country of Ireland.
237	Et qant il sont al port venu,	And when it they to-the-port came,	And when they had come into harbour,
238	Melïon n'a plus atendu,	Melion could-not more wait,	Melion waited no longer;
239	Ains issi fors de son cloier,	Rather thus out of his enclosure,	He came out from his bench
240	De la nef sailli el gravier.	Of there the-ship leapt he to-the-ground.	And leapt from the boat on to the shingle.
241	Li maronier l'ont escrié	The mariners to-him-they shouted	The sailors shouted at him

Melion

	Old French	Literal	English
242	*Et de lor aviron geté.*	And of their oars threw.	And threw their oars at him.
243	*Li uns l'a d'un baston feru,*	Of-them one his of-a stick struck,	One of them struck him with a stick
244	*A poi k'il ne l'ont retenu;*	And little could-he not they catch;	And they nearly managed to catch him;
245	*Lies est qant lor fu escapés.*	Happy he-was when from-them became escaped.	He was glad when he had escaped from them.
246	*Sor une montaigne est alés;*	Upon a mountain he went;	He went up a mountain
247	*Molt a regardé le païs*	Much he looked-at the country	And looked closely at the country
248	*Ou il savoit ses anemis.*	Where he knew his enemies.	Where he knew his enemies to be.
249	*Encore avoit il son lardé*	Still had he his piece-of-meat	He still had his piece of meat,
250	*Ke de sa terre ot aporté;*	Which of his country had carried;	Which he had brought from his own land;
251	*Grant faim avoit, si l'a mangié,*	Great hunger had, so he ate,	He was very hungry, so he ate it,
252	*Molt l'avoit la mer traveillié.*	Much had the sea exhausted.	The sea crossing had exhausted him.
253	*En une forest est alés,*	He a forest was went-to,	He went into a forest,
254	*Vaches et bues i a trovés.*	Cows and oxen there he found.	And found cows and oxen there.
255	*Molt en ocit et estrangla;*	Many of-them killed and strangled;	He killed and strangled many of them;
256	*Iluec sa guerre comencha.*	There his war began.	There he began his war.
257	*Plus en i a ocis de cent*	More of he had killed than a-hundred	He killed more than a hundred of them
258	*A cest premier commencement.*	At this early stage.	At this early stage.
259	*La gent ki estoit el boscage*	There people who were in the-woods	The people who lived in the woodland
260	*Virent des bestes le damage;*	Saw of-them beasts he harmed;	Saw their beasts harmed;
261	*Corant vindrent a la cité,*	Running they-went to the city,	They went running to the city,
262	*Al roi l'ont dit et aconté*	To-the king they said and recounted	Spoke to the king and said
263	*Qu'en la forest .I. leu avoit*	which there forest a wolf was	That there was a wolf in the forest,

Melion

	Old French	Literal	English
264	Ki le païs tot escilloit.	Which the land all ravaged.	Which was ravaging all the land.
265	Molt a ocis de lor almaille;	Many of killed of their animals;	It had killed many of their livestock;
266	Mais tot ce tient li rois a faille.	But all this thought the king of failed.	But all this thought the king nothing of.
267	Tant a alé par la forest,	So-much had gone by the forest,	Melion went so far through the forest,
268	Par montaignes et par dessert,	By mountains and by wasteland,	Through the mountains and the wasteland,
269	Que a .X. leus s'acompaigna:	That was Ten wolves accompanied:	That he was joined by ten wolves;
270	Tant les blandi et losenga	So-much he cajoled and persuaded	He cajoled and persuaded them so much
271	Que avoec lui les a menés,	That with him he had taken,	That he took them with him
272	Et font totes ses volentés.	And they-did all he wished.	And they did all he wished.
273	Par le païs molt se forvoient,	By the countryside much they went,	They went roaming through the countryside
274	Homes et femes malmenoient.	Men and women attacked.	And attacked men and women.
275	Un an tot plain ont si esté:	One year all full they thus were:	For a full year they were like this:
276	Tot le païs ont degasté,	All the country they laid-waste,	They laid waste all the country,
277	Homes et femes ocioient;	Men and women killed;	Killed men and women
278	Tote la terre destruioient.	All the land destroyed.	And destroyed all the land.
279	Molt se savoient bien gaitier;	Very-much they knew well protect;	They knew how to protect themselves well;
280	Li rois nes pooit engingnier.	The king not could trick.	The king could not trick them.
281	Une nuit orent molt erré,	One night had-they much roamed,	One night they had roamed widely
282	Traveillié furent et pené.	Exhausted they-were and weary.	And were exhausted and wearied.
283	En .I. bois joste Duveline,	In one forest next-to Dublin,	There was a wood near Dublin,
284	Sor .I. tertre les la marine -	On a mound by the sea	On a mound next to the sea
285	Li bois estoit les une plaigne	The wood was by a plain	The wood was near a plain,

Melion

	Old French	Literal	English
286	Tot environ ot grant compaigne -	Completely surrounded with large fields	Completely surrounded by open countryside
287	Por reposer i sont entré.	For rest there they entered.	And they entered it to rest themselves.
288	Traï seront et engané:	Betrayed the-will-be and tricked:	They will be betrayed and tricked:
289	Un païsant les a veüs;	One peasant them of saw;	A peasant saw them,
290	Al roi en est tantost corus.	To the-king then was immediately ran.	And at once ran to the king.
291	'Sire', dist il, 'el bois reont	'Sire', said he, 'in the-forest round	'Sire', he said, 'in the round wood
292	Li .XI. leu colchié s'i sont.'	They eleven wolves laid-up they are'.	The eleven wolves have laid up'.
293	Qant li rois l'ot, molt en fu liés;	When the king heard, much he became happy;	When the king heard it, he was very glad,
294	Ses homes en a araisniés.	His men he had called.	And he addressed his men.
295	Li rois ses homes apela.	The king his men addressed.	The king called his men.
296	'Baron', dist il, 'entendés cha!	'Barons', said he, 'listen to-me	'Barons', he said, 'listen to me.
297	Sachiés de voir les .XI. lous	Know-you the truth this eleven wolves	Know in truth that this man here
298	En ma forest vit cis hom tous.'	In my forest saw this man all'.	Has seen all eleven wolves in my forest'.
299	Les rois dont soelent les pors prandre	The nets they-had only the boars to-catch	They had the nets, which they used to capture boar
300	Environ le bois ont fait tendre.	Around the forest they were out-stretched.	Stretched around the woods.
301	Qant on les ot tot portendus,	When they the with all stretched-out,	When they had been all stretched out,
302	Lors monta, n'i atarga plus.	He mounted, not delaying more.	He mounted and did not delay any longer.
303	Sa fille dist avoec venra	His daughter said with would-go	His daughter said she would go with him
304	Et la chace des leus verra.	And the hunting of-the wolves watch.	And watch the hunting of the wolves.
305	Tantost se sont el bois alé,	Immediately of they the woods went,	At once they went to the wood,
306	Tot coiement et a celé;	All secretly and of hidden;	In complete secrecy and well hidden;
307	Le bois ont tot avironé,	The forest they all surrounded,	They surrounded the wood completely,

Melion

	Old French	Literal	English
308	*Car gent i ot a grant plenté*	Because people there with was a-great many	For there were a great many people
309	*Ki portent haces et maçues,*	Who carried axes and cudgels,	Who carried axes and cudgels,
310	*Et li alqant espees nues.*	And they some swords bared.	And some had swords bared.
311	*Adont i ot .M. chiens hués*	Now there with A-thousand hounds excited	Now there were a thousand excited hounds,
312	*Ki les leus orent tost trovés.*	Which the wolves heard immediately found.	Which quickly found the wolves.
313	*Melïon vit k'il ert traïs:*	Melion saw that-he was betrayed:	Melion saw that he was betrayed:
314	*Bien set que il est malbaillis.*	Well knew that he was in-trouble.	He understood that he was in trouble.
315	*Li chien les vont molt angoissant*	The dogs they went very aggressively	The dogs went for them viciously
316	*Et il vienent as rois fuiant.*	And they came in the-nets running.	And they came fleeing into the nets.
317	*Tot sont detrancié et ocis;*	All were cut-up and killed;	All were cut to pieces and killed;
318	*Un tos seus n'en escapa vis*	One all single not escape knew	Not a single one of them escaped alive,
319	*Fors Melïon, qui escapa,*	Except Melion, who escaped,	Save for Melion, who fled
320	*Par deseure les rois lança.*	By only the nets leaping.	By leaping over the nets.
321	*En .I. grant bois s'en est alé;*	Then a great wood he was gone;	He went into a great wood;
322	*Par engien lor est escapé.*	By ingenuity his had escaped.	He had escaped by his ingenuity.
323	*A la cité sont repairié;*	To the city they went;	The hunters went back to the city;
324	*Li rois se fait durement lié.*	The king he became very pleased.	The king was very pleased.
325	*Li rois grant joie demena*	The king great joy took	The king felt great joy
326	*Que il des .XI. leus .X. a,*	That he of eleven wolves Ten had,	That he had ten of the eleven wolves,
327	*Car molt bien s'est vengié des leus;*	For very well he avenged of-the wolves;	So he had avenged himself well on the wolves:
328	*Escapés ne l'en est c'uns seus.*	Escaped only of-them was one alone.	Only one of them alone had escaped.
329	*Sa fille dist: 'C'est li plus grans;*	His daughter said: 'this he most large;	His daughter said: 'This one was the largest;

Melion

	Old French	Literal	English
330	*Encor les fera tos dolans'.*	Still he will-make all regret.	He will still make them all regret it'.
331	*Qant Melïon fu escapés,*	When Melion had escaped,	When Melion had escaped,
332	*Sor une montaigne est montés;*	Over a mountain he mounted;	He climbed a mountain;
333	*Molt fu dolans, molt li pesa*	Much became unhappy, much he-was troubled	He was very unhappy and troubled
334	*De ses leus que il perdu a.*	Of his wolves which he lost had.	About his wolves, which he had lost.
335	*Molt a traveillié longement,*	Much had-he suffered a-long-time,	For a long time he had suffered,
336	*Mais ore avra socors briement:*	But soon will-he-have help shortly:	But in a short while now he will have help:
337	*Artus en Yrlande venoit,*	Arthur to Ireland came,	Arthur was coming to Ireland,
338	*Car une pais faire i voloit.*	Because a peace-treaty to-make he wished.	For he wished to make a peace treaty.
339	*Mellé estoient el païs,*	Conflicts there-were in the-land,	There were conflicts in the land
340	*Acorder vout les anemis.*	Agreement wished he to-bring.	And he wished to bring agreement to the factions;
341	*Sor les Romains voloit conquerre;*	Over the Romans he-wanted-to conquer;	He wanted to conquer the Romans,
342	*Mener les voloit en sa guerre.*	To-take them he-wished to this war.	He wanted to lead them in his war.
343	*Li rois venoit priveement,*	The king went privately,	The king was travelling privately,
344	*Ne menoit mie molt grant gent:*	Not many at-all many great people:	He did not bring very many people;
345	*.XX. chevaliers od lui menoit.*	twenty knights with him brought.	He brought with him twenty knights.
346	*Molt fist bel tans, bon vent avoit,*	Very-much was well the-weather, good wind had,	The weather was fine, they had a good wind;
347	*Molt fu la nef et riche et grans.*	Many became there ship and splendid and large.	The ship was both splendid and large
348	*Il i avoit bons esturmans;*	He with had good steersman;	And there was a good steersman;
349	*Molt par fu bien apareillie,*	Very-well by was well equipped,	It was very well equipped
350	*D'ommes et d'armes bien garnie.*	of-men and arms well supplied.	And supplied with men and arms.
351	*Lor escus furent fors pendus.*	Their shields were outside hanging.	Their shields were hung over the side.

Melion

	Old French	Literal	English
352	Melïons les a coneüs.	Melion them of recognised.	Melion recognised them.
353	Primes conut l'escu Gawain	First recognised the-shield Gawain's	First he recognised Gawain's shield,
354	Et puis a ravisé l'Iwain	And then he noticed Yvain's	And then he noticed Yvain's,
355	Et puis l'escu le roi Ydel;	And then the-shield the king Ydel;	And then King Ydel's shield;
356	Tot ce li plot et li fu bel.	All this him delighted and he became pleased.	All this delighted him and was pleasing to him.
357	L'escu le roi bien ravisa;	the-shield the king's well recognised;	He recognised the king's shield easily;
358	Sachiés de voir grant joie en a.	Knew of truly greay joy he had.	Know truly that he was very joyful because of this:
359	Molt en fu liés, molt s'esjoï,	Very was he happy, much rejoicing,	He was very happy about it and rejoiced greatly,
360	Car encor quide avoir merci.	Because still believed have mercy.	For he believed he would have mercy.
361	Vers la terre vienent siglant,	Towards the land they-came sailing,	They came sailing towards the land,
362	Li vens lor est venus devant,	But the-wind them was veering before,	But the wind veered in front of them.
363	Ne porent prendre cil le port;	Not could take they the harbour;	They could not reach the harbour;
364	Adont i ot grant desconfort.	Thus he had great discomfort.	Now Melion had great despair.
365	A .I. autre port sont torné,	Then An other port they turned-to,	They turned towards another port,
366	A .II. lieues de la cité.	That two leagues from the city.	Two leagues from the city.
367	Un grant castel i ot jadis,	One great castle there was in-days-passed,	Once there was a great castle there,
368	Mais ore estoit tos agastis,	But now was all ruined,	But now it was all ruined,
369	Et qant il furent arivé	And when they had arrived	And when they arrived
370	Nuis estoit, si ert avespré.	Night was, and was dark.	It was night, it was dark.
371	Li rois s'est al port arivés.	The king he-was to-the port arrived.	The king reached the port.
372	Molt s'est traveilliés et penés	Very-much he-was tired and suffering	He was very tired and suffering
373	Car la nef li ot fait grant mal.	Because the ship him had made very ill.	Because the ship him had made very ill.

Melion

	Old French	Literal	English
374	Il apela son senescal.	He called his steward.	He called his steward.
375	'Alés', dist il, 'la fors veïr	'Go', said he, 'there outside see	'Go', he said, 'and see out there
376	U jo porrai anuit gesir.'	Where I could tonight lie'.	Where I can sleep tonight'.
377	Cil est a la nef retornés;	He was to there the-ship returned;	Then he went back to the ship
378	Les canberlens a apelés.	The chamberlains he called.	And called the chamberlains.
379	'Issiés', fait il, 'ça fors od moi,	'Come', do it, 'thus outside with me,	'Come on land with me', he said,
380	Si atornés l'ostel le roi.'	Thus prepare lodging the king'.	And prepare lodging for the king'.
381	Fors de la nef en sont issu,	Outside of the ship of they went,	Outside of the ship of they went,
382	Si en sont a l'ostel venu.	This with went to lodging went.	And came to the lodging.
383	.II. chierges i ont fait porter,	two torches there they had carried,	They had two torches carried there
384	Molt tost les firent alumer.	Very quickly them had illuminated.	And quickly had them illuminated.
385	Kieutes i portent et tapis,	Quilts they carried and carpets,	They carried quilts and carpets
386	Hastivement fu bien garnis.	Quickly preparing well furnishing.	And quickly prepared furnishings well.
387	Adont s'en est li rois issus;	Thus then was the king left;	Then the king left the ship
388	Droit a l'ostel en est venus,	Straight to lodging then was came,	And came straight to the lodging,
389	Et qant il i fu ens entré	And when he there became in entered	And when he had gone in
390	Liés est qant si bel l'a trové.	Happy was when thus well this found.	He was glad to find it all so pleasant.
391	Melïons pas ne se targa:	Melion not no-longer he delayed:	Melion did not hesitate:
392	Tostans contre la nef ala.	Went towards the ship along.	He went at once towards the ship.
393	Pres de la chasvie est arestus;	Close of the castle he stopped;	He halted near the castle
394	Molt les a bien reconeüs.	Very-much they he well recognised.	And recognised them very well.
395	Bien set se del roi n'a confort	Well knew he of the-king not-having comfort	He well knew, if he had no comfort from the king,

Melion

	Old French	Literal	English
396	Qu'en Yrlande prendra la mort.	that-in Ireland would there die.	That he would die in Ireland;
397	Mais il ne set comment aler,	But he not knew how-to proceed,	But he did not know how to proceed:
398	Leus est et si ne set parler.	Wolf was and thus not knew speech.	He was a wolf and could not speak.
399	Et nekedent tostans ira,	And nevertheless went-forwards at-once,	Nevertheless he would go forward at once,
400	En aventure se metra.	And risked his life.	And risk his life.
401	A l'uis le roi en est venus;	Then he-came-to the king and was come;	He came to the king's door;
402	Tot ses barons a coneüs.	All the barons he recognised.	He knew all the barons.
403	Il ne s'est de rien arestés;	He not was of nothing stopping;	He did not stop for a moment,
404	Tot droit al roi en est alés,	All directly to-the king was he went,	But went directly up to the king,
405	En aventure est de morir.	And risked he of death.	Although it might mean his death.
406	As piés le roi se lait chaïr,	At the-feet the king he had fallen,	He let himself fall at the king's feet
407	Ne se voloit pas redrecier;	Not he wished not to-get-up;	And would not rise again;
408	Dont la veïsciés merveillier.	Then there would-have-seen amazement.	Then you would have seen amazement there.
409	Ce dist li rois: 'Merveilles voi!	This said the king: 'Marvels I-see	The king spoke thus: 'I can see marvels!
410	Cis leus est ci venus a moi.	The wolf has here come to me.	This wolf has come here to me.
411	Or sachiés bien qu'il est privés.	Now know well which is tame.	Now know well that he is tame.
412	Mar ert touchiés ne adesés.'	Wrongly to touch or approach'.	Wrong to anyone who touches or approaches him'.
413	Qant li mangier sont apresté	When the meal was ready	When the meal was ready,
414	Et li barons orent lavé,	And the barons soon washed,	And the barons soon washed,
415	Li rois lava, si s'est assis;	The king washed, thus was seated;	And the king washed and sat down;
416	Devant ax ont les dobliers mis.	In-front to-the they the plates set.	The dishes were placed before them.
417	Li rois a Ydel apelé,	The king to Ydel called,	The king called to Ydel

Melion

	Old French	Literal	English
418	*Se l'assist joste son costé.*	He seated next-to his side.	And sat him at his side.
419	*As piés le roi jut Melïons;*	At feet the king's lay Melion;	Melion lay at the king's feet
420	*Bien conut trestot les barons.*	Well recognised all the barons.	And recognised all the barons well.
421	*Li rois le regarda sovent.*	The king him glanced-at often.	The king glanced at him often.
422	*Un pain li done et il le prent,*	One piece-of-bread he gave and he it received,	He gave Melion a piece of bread and he took it;
423	*Puis le commença a mangier.*	Then he began to eat.	Then he began to eat it.
424	*Li rois s'en prist a merveillier;*	The king was seized with marvel;	The king began to marvel at this;
425	*Al roi Ydel dist: 'Esgardés!*	To-the king Ydel said: 'Look!	He said to King Ydel: 'Look!
426	*Sachiés que cis leus est privés'.*	Know-you that this wolf is tame.	You can be sure this wolf is tame'.
427	*Li rois .I. lardé li dona*	The king one piece-of-meat him gave	The king gave Melion a piece of meat
428	*Et il volentiers le manga.*	And it gladly he ate.	And he ate it gladly.
429	*Lors dist Gavains: 'Segnor, veés;*	Then said Gawain: 'My-lords, look;	Then Gawain said: 'My lords, look;
430	*Cis leus est tous desnaturés'.*	This wolf is completely unnatural.	This wolf is completely unnatural'.
431	*Entr'aus dïent tot li baron*	amongst said all the barons	All the barons said amongst themselves
432	*C'ainc si cortois leu ne vit on.*	as-this so courteous a-wolf not seen one.	That no-one had never seen such a well-mannered wolf.
433	*Li rois fait aporter le vin*	The king had brought him wine	The king had wine brought
434	*Devant le leu en .I. bacin.*	Before the wolf in a basin.	Before the wolf in a basin.
435	*Li leus le voit, beüt en a;*	The wolf this saw, drank of it;	The wolf saw it and drank some;
436	*Sachiés que molt le desira*	Know-you that much he desired	You may be sure he wanted it very much,
437	*Qu'il a del vin assés beü,*	which he from wine well drank,	For he drank deeply of the wine,
438	*Et li rois l'a molt bien veü.*	And the king this very well watched.	And the king watched him closely.
439	*Qant del mangier furent levé*	When from the-meal had risen	When they had risen from the meal

Melion

	Old French	Literal	English
440	Et li baron orent lavé,	And the barons now washed,	And the barons had washed,
441	Fors issirent sor le gravoi.	Outside they-went to the shore.	They went out on to the shore.
442	Tostans fu li leus ot le roi;	Always was the wolf with the king;	The wolf was always with the king;
443	Onques ne sot cel lieu aler	Never not knew the place to-go	He did not know anywhere he could go
444	C'on le peüst de lui oster.	where he could of him separate.	Where he could be separated from him.
445	Qant li rois volt aler colchier,	When the king wanted to-go retire,	When the king wanted to retire,
446	Son lit rova apareillier.	His bed ordered prepared.	He ordered his bed to be prepared;
447	Dormir s'en vait, molt est lassés,	To-sleep then went, very much tired,	He went to sleep, he was very tired,
448	Et li leus est od lui alés,	And the wolf was with him went,	And the wolf went with him;
449	Ainc nel pot on de li partir,	Rather none could they of him leave,	No-one could make him leave him;
450	As piés le roi en vait gesir.	At the-feet the king's then went to-lie.	He went to lie at the king's feet.
451	Li rois d'Yrlande a mes eüs	The king of-Ireland had message of-them	The King of Ireland received a message
452	C'Artus estoit a lui venus;	That-Arthur was to him come;	That Arthur had come to him;
453	Molt en fu liés, grant joie en a.	Very-much he became glad, greatly rejoiced then he.	He was very glad and rejoiced greatly.
454	Bien main a l'aube se leva,	Well morning at dawn he rose,	He rose very early at dawn
455	Deci al port en est alés;	Went to-the harbour then he went;	And went to the harbour,
456	Ses barons a o lui menés,	His barons he with him took,	Taking his barons with him;
457	Tot droit al port en vint errant.	All directly to-the-harbour then came were.	They all made directly for the harbour.
458	Molt s'entrefirent bel samblant;	Much greeting well mannered;	They greeted each other in a friendly manner;
459	Artus li mostra grant amor	Arthur him showed great love	Arthur showed him great love
460	Et fait li a molt grant honor.	And did him a very great honour.	And did him great honour.
461	Qant il le voit a lui venir,	When he him saw the king coming,	When he saw the King of Ireland coming towards him,

Melion

	Old French	Literal	English
462	*Ne se volt mie enorgoillir,*	Not he wished not-at-all haughty,	He did not wish to appear haughty,
463	*Ains leva sus, si l'a baisié.*	Rather stood up, thus him embraced.	But stood up and embraced him.
464	*Li ceval sont apareillié;*	The horses were prepared;	The horses were ready;
465	*Ne targent plus, ains sont monté,*	Not delayed more, rather they mounted,	They delayed no longer, but mounted,
466	*Ore en iront vers la cité.*	Now them rode towards the city.	Then rode them towards the city.
467	*Li rois monte en son palefroi,*	The king mounted then his palfrey,	The king mounted his palfrey
468	*Se son leu a pris bon conroi.*	He his wolf then took good care-of.	And took good care of his wolf;
469	*Ne le voloit mie laissier;*	Not he wished not-at-all to-leave;	He did not wish to leave him behind.
470	*Il fu tos jors a son estrier.*	He became all day at his stirrup.	All the time Melion was at his stirrup.
471	*D'Artus fu molt li rois joians,*	Arthur became very-much the king joyed,	The king was very happy to see Arthur,
472	*Li conrois fu riches et grans.*	The company was splendid and large.	The company was large and magnificent.
473	*A Duveline sont venu*	To Dublin they came	They came to Dublin
474	*Et el grant palais descendu.*	And in great palace dismounted..	And dismounted at the great palace.
475	*Qant li rois monta el doignon,*	When the king went-up in the-keep,	When the king went up into the keep,
476	*Li leus li tint par le giron;*	The wolf him went by his robe;	The wolf held him by the skirt of his robe;
477	*Qant li rois Artus fu assis,*	When the king Arthur was seated,	When King Arthur was seated,
478	*Li leus s'est a ses piés mis.*	The wolf was by his feet set.	The wolf placed himself at his feet.
479	*Li rois a son leu regardé;*	The king to his wolf looked;	The king looked at his wolf;
480	*Joste le dois l'a apelé.*	Close he must be called.	He called him near to the table.
481	*Ensamble sisent li doi roi,*	Together sat the two kings,	The two kings sat together;
482	*Molt par i ot riche conroi,*	Very-much by there with splendid company,	The company was splendid,
483	*Molt bien servoient li baron;*	Very well served the barons;	The barons waited on them very well:

Melion

	Old French	Literal	English
484	De totes pars par la maison	Of all parts by the dwelling	In all parts of the dwelling
485	Servi furent a grant plenté.	Served were a great plenty.	They were served lavishly.
486	Mais Melïon a regardé;	But Melion around looked;	But Melion looked around;
487	Enmi la sale ravisa	In-the-middle there hall noticed	He noticed in the middle of the hall
488	Celui ki sa feme enmena.	He who had wife-his taken-away.	The man his wife had taken away with her.
489	Bien sot la mer estoit passés	Well knew the sea was crossed	He knew that he had crossed the sea
490	Et en Yrlande estoit alés.	And in Ireland was gone.	And had gone to Ireland.
491	Par l'espaule le vait saisir:	By his-shoulder he went to-seize:	He went to seize him by the shoulder:
492	Cil ne se pot a lui tenir;	He not him could off him hold;	The man could not keep him at bay;
493	En la sale l'a abatu.	In the hall he attacked.	Melion attacked him in the hall:
494	Ja l'eüst mort et confondu,	Already would-have killed him destroyed,	He would have soon killed and destroyed him
495	Ne fuissent li sergant le roi	Not was-it-not-for the servants the king's	Had it not been for the king's servants,
496	Qui la vindrent a grant desroi;	Who there saw the great commotion;	Who saw the great commotion;
497	De totes pars par le palais	From all parts by the palace	From all parts of the palace
498	Fus aporterent et gamais.	Were brought and sticks.	They carried sticks and cudgels.
499	Ja eüsent le leu tué,	Already would-have the wolf killed,	They would certainly have killed the wolf
500	Qant li rois Artus a crié,	When the king Arthur he cried,	When King Arthur cried out:
501	'Mar ert touchiés', fait il, 'par foi!	'Wrong who touches, does him, 'by faith!	'Wrong to anyone who touches him', he said, 'by my faith!
502	Sachiés que li leus est a moi'.	Know-you that the wolf is of mine.	Know that this wolf is mine'.
503	Dist Ydel, li fiex Yrïen:	Said Ydel, the son-of Yrien:	Ydel, son of Yrien, said:
504	'Segnor, ne faites mie bien;	'My-lords, not doing not-at-all well;	'My lords, you are not doing right at all;
505	S'il nel haïst, nel touchast pas',	if-he did-not hate-him, nor touched-him not,	If the wolf had not hated him, he would not have touched him',

Melion

	Old French	Literal	English
506	*Et dist li rois: 'Ydel, droit as'.*	And said the king: 'Ydel, right is.	And the king said: 'Ydel, you are right'.
507	*Artus s'en est del dois tornés;*	Arthur then was from the-table turned-away;	Arthur moved away from the table,
508	*Deci al leu en est alés,*	And-then to-the wolf then he went,	And went right up to the wolf.
509	*Al vallet dist: 'Tu jehiras*	To-the servant said: 'You-will confess	He said to the servant: 'You will confess
510	*Porcoi t'a pris ou ja morras'.*	Why you-he seized or at-once die.	Why he seized you or you shall die at once'.
511	*Melïons le roi regarda;*	Melion the king looked-at;	Melion looked at the king;
512	*Celui estraint et il cria.*	He gripped and he cried-out.	He gripped the servant and he cried out.
513	*Cil a le roi merci rové;*	He then the king's mercy begged;	He begged the king for mercy,
514	*Dist k'il contera verité.*	Saying that-he would-recount the-truth.	Saying that he would tell him the truth.
515	*Maintenant a le roi conté*	At-once he the king recounted	At once he told the king
516	*Comment la dame l'ot mené,*	How the lady before he-took,	How the lady had brought him with her,
517	*Comment del anel le toucha*	How of-the ring she touched	How she had touched Melion with the ring,
518	*Et en Yrlande l'en mena.*	And then Ireland him-there took.	And taken him there to Ireland.
519	*Tot li a dit et coneü*	All he had said and made-known	All this he said and made known,
520	*Comment li estoit avenu.*	Just as it-was happened.	Just as it had happened.
521	*Artus a le roi apelé:*	Arthur then the king called:	Arthur addressed the King of Ireland,
522	*'Or sai bien que c'est verité;*	'Now I-know well that it-is true;	'Now I know well that this is true;
523	*De mon baron m'est il molt bel.*	Of my baron mine-is he very-much beloved.	I am very happy about my baron.
524	*Faites moi delivrer l'anel*	Have to-me brought the-ring	Have the ring brought to me
525	*Et vo fille, ki l'enporta;*	And your daughter, which it-took-away;	And your daughter, who took it away;
526	*Malvaisement engignié l'a.'*	Evil tricked she-has'.	She has played an evil trick on him'.
527	*Li rois s'en est d'iluec tornés,*	The king then was from-there turned-away,	The King of Ireland left there;

Melion

	Old French	Literal	English
528	En sa cambre s'en est entrés;	To his chamber then he entered;	He went into his chamber,
529	Le roi Ydel o lui mena.	The kinf Ydel with him took.	Taking King Ydel with him.
530	Tant le blandi et losenga	So-much he cajoled and persuaded	He cajoled and persuaded his daughter so much
531	Qu'ele li a l'anel doné;	that-she to-him then the-ring gave;	That she gave him the ring;
532	Il l'a al roi Artu porté.	He this to-the king Arthur brought.	He brought it to King Arthur.
533	Si tost con l'anel a veü,	As soon-as recognised the-ring he saw,	As soon as he saw the ring,
534	Melïon l'a bien coneü;	Melion this well recognised;	Melion recognised it well;
535	Al roi vint, si s'agenoilla	To-the king went, so kneeling	He went to the king, fell on his knees
536	Et andeus les pies li baisa.	And both his feet he kissed.	And kissed both his feet.
537	Li rois Artus le vout touchier;	The king Arthur him wanted to-touch;	King Arthur wanted to touch him,
538	Gavains nel volt pas otroier.	Gawain not willed not agree-to.	But Gawain would not permit it.
539	'Biaus oncles', fait il, 'non ferés!	'Good uncle, said he, 'don't do	'Good uncle', he said, 'don't!
540	En une chambre l'en menrés,	Into a chamber him take,	Take him to a chamber
541	Tot seul a seul priveement,	All alone by himself privately,	In absolute privacy
542	Que il n'ait honte de la gent'.	That he is-not shamed of the people.	So that he is not shamed in front of people'.
543	Li rois a Gavain apelé,	The king of Gawain called,	The king called Gawain,
544	Si a od lui Ydel mené,	And he with him Ydel took,	And he took Ydel with him;
545	En une cambre l'en mena.	To a chamber he-him took.	He led Melion to a chamber.
546	Qant il fu ens, l'uis si ferma,	When he was inside, was thus closed,	When he was inside, he closed the door.
547	L'anel li a sor le chief mis;	the-ring he to above his head set;	He put the ring to Melion's head;
548	D'ome li aparut le vis,	of-a-man to-him appeared his face,	His face appeared like a man's,
549	Tote sa figure mua.	All his person mutated.	All his body changed.

Melion

	Old French	Literal	English
550	Lors devint hom et si parla.	Then became man and then spoke.	Then he became a man and spoke.
551	As pies le roi se lait cheïr;	At-the feet-of the king he then fell;	He let himself fall at the king's feet;
552	D'un mantel le firent covrir.	of-a mantle he-was made covered.	They wrapped him in a cloak.
553	Qant le virent home formé,	When this they-saw the-man formed,	When they saw him shaped as a man,
554	Molt ont grant joie demené.	Many they great joy took.	They felt very great joy.
555	De pitié li rois en plora,	Of pity the king then wept,	The king wept for pity over him
556	Et en plorant li demanda	And in weeping him asked	And weeping asked him
557	Comment li estoit avenu,	How it was happened,	How this had happened to him;
558	Par pechié l'avoient perdu.	By misfortune had lost.	Through misfortune they had lost him.
559	Son canberlenc a fait mander,	His chamberlain he had called-for,	He had his chamberlain sent for,
560	Riches dras li fist aporter;	Rich clothes he had brought;	And had rich clothing brought to him;
561	Bien le vesti et conrea	Well he dressed and cultivated	He dressed Melion and turned him out well
562	Et en la sale le mena.	And in the hall they took.	And took him into the hall.
563	Merveillié sont par la maison	Marvel they by the dwelling	Throughout the dwelling they marvelled
564	Qant voient venir Melïon.	When they-saw coming Melion.	When they saw Melion coming.
565	Li rois a sa fille amenee.	The king then his daughter brought.	The king brought his daughter.
566	Al roi Artus l'a presentee,	To-the king Arthur he presented,	He presented her to King Arthur,
567	A tote sa volenté faire,	As all how he-wished to-do,	To do with as he wished,
568	Voille l'ardoir, voille desfaire.	Wishing torn-to-pieces, wishing to-do.	Whether to burn her or have her torn to pieces.
569	Melïons dist: 'Jel toucherai	Melion said: 'I shall-touch	Melion said: 'I shall touch her
570	De la piere, ja nel lairai'.	Of the stone, me nothing shall-stop.	With the stone, nothing will stop me'.
571	Artus li a dit: 'Non ferés!	Arthur to-him then said: 'Don't do!	Arthur said to him: 'Don't!

Melion

	Old French	Literal	English
572	*Por vos beaus enfans le lairés.'*	For your beautiful children her let-be'.	For the sake of your beautiful children, let her be'.
573	*Tot li baron l'en ont proié;*	All the barons him they begged;	All the barons begged it of him;
574	*Melïon lor a otroié.*	Melion their of granted.	Melion granted their wish.
575	*Li rois Artus tant demora*	The king Arthur until delayed	Arthur remained there
576	*Que la guerre tot acorda.*	When the war was-all in-accord.	Until the war was settled.
577	*En sa contree en est alés,*	Then his country he was going,	Then he set out for his own land,
578	*Melïon a od lui menés;*	Melion then with him took;	Taking Melion with him;
579	*Molt en fu liés, grant joie en a.*	Very-much he became glad, great joy at it.	Melion was very glad, he rejoiced at it.
580	*Sa feme en Yrlande laissa:*	His wife in Ireland he-left:	He left his wife in Ireland.
581	*A deables l'a commandee;*	To the-devil he-her commended;	He commended her to the devil;
582	*Jamais n'iert jor de li amee,*	Never another day of he loved,	She would never again be loved by him
583	*Por ce qu'ele l'ot si bailli,*	Because that which-she before so burdened,	Because she had mistreated him so badly,
584	*Con vos avés el conte oï.*	As you have in the-recounting heard.	As you have heard in the tale.
585	*Ne le volt il onques reprendre,*	No-longer her willed he never take-back,	He never wished to take her back,
586	*Ains le laissast ardoir u pendre.*	Rather her let-be burned or hanged.	He would like to have let her burn or be dismembered.
587	*Melïon dist: 'Ja ne faldra*	Melion said: 'Indeed never fail	Melion said: 'It will never fail to happen
588	*Que de tot sa feme kerra,*	Which of completely his wife believes,	That he who believes his wife completely
589	*Qu'en la fin ne soit malbaillis;*	will there end he let-be badly-done;	Will be ruined in the end;
590	*Ne doit pas croire tos ses dis'.*	He should not believe all she says.	He should not believe all she says'.
591	*Vrais est li lais de Melïon,*	True is the lay of Melion,	The Lay of Melion is true,
592	*Ce dïent bien tot li baron.*	So they-say well all the barons.	As all the nobles say.
593	*Explicit de Melïon*	Now-is-the-end of Melion	This is the end of Melion.

Melion

Old French	Literal	English
594 *Chi fine Melïon*	Here ends Melion	Here ends Melion.

Word List (Old French to English)

Old French	English

0-9

A, a

Old French	English
a	a, against, and, around, as, at, by, had, had-he, has, he, in, is, it, of, off, on, that, the, then, this, to, under, up to, was, with
abatu	attacked, brought-down
aconté	recounted
acorda	in-accord
acorder	agreement
adesé	approached
adesés	approach
adont	now, thus
afublez	wrapped
agastis	ruined
ai	have, have-I
ainc	earlier, rather
ains	earlier, rather
aïtant	at-this-point
al	at, in, of, the, to, to-the
ala	along, go, he-went, of, of-the, went
alé	going, gone, went
aler	go, proceed, to-go
alés	go, going, gone, went, went-to
almaille	animals
alqant	some
alques	somewhat
altre	other
alumer	illuminated
ama	he-loved
amé	loved
amee	loved
amenee	brought
amer	love, loved, to-love
amerai	shall-I-love
amont	up
amor	love
an	year
anchois	in-choice
andeus	both
anel	ring
anemis	enemies, to-bring
angoissant	aggressively
ans	years
antendu	heard
anuit	tonight
anuita	night-fall
apareillie	equipped
apareillié	prepared
apareillier	prepared
aparut	appeared
apela	addressed, called, he-called
apelé	called
apelés	called
aporté	carried
aporter	brought
aporterai	I-shall-bring
aporterent	brought
apresté	ready
araisniés	called
ardoir	burn, burned
arestés	stopping
arestus	stopped
arivé	arrived
arivés	arrived
artu	Arthur (a name)
artus	Arthur (a name)
as	at, at-the, have, in, is, the, you
asopli	downcast
assés	many, much, very well, very-well, well
assez	rather
assis	seated
atarga	delaying
atendi	waited, waiting

Word List (Old French to English)

Old French	English
atendu	attended, wait
atorna	returned
atornés	prepare
auroit	have
autre	other
avant	forward, further
aventure	adventure, risked
avenu	happened
avés	have
avespra	evening-fell
avespré	dark
aviron	oars
avironé	surrounded
avoec	with
avoient	they-had
avoir	be, have
avoit	had, he-had, was
avra	has, will-he-have
ax	to-the

Æ, æ

B, b

Old French	English
bacheler	knight, page, young knight aspirant, young man
bacin	basin
bailli	burdened
baisa	kissed
baisie	kissed
baisié	embraced
baissié	lowered
baron	baron, barons, brave knight, brave warrior
barons	barons
baston	stick
beaus	beautiful
beax	beautiful
bel	beautiful, beloved, dear, handsome, pleased, well
bele	beautiful, beauty, elegant, fair-lady
belement	politely
bercerië	quiver
bestes	beasts
beü	drank
beüt	drank
biaus	good
bien	good, good fortune, many, much, really, well, well-being
blance	white
blandi	cajoled
blonde	blonde
bois	forest, forests, the-forest, tree, wood, woods
bon	fair, good
bone	good
bons	good
bonté	excellence
boscage	the-woods
bouche	mouth
briement	shortly
bues	oxen
buisson	bush

C, c

Old French	English
c	a-hundred
c'ainc	as-this
cambre	chamber
canberlenc	chamberlain
canberlens	chamberlains
canbres	chambers
car	because, for
c'artus	that-Arthur
cascuns	each
castel	castle
caston	casting
ce	he, it, so, that, this
cel	that, the, this
cele	such, that, that-time, the, this
celé	hidden
celes	hide, those
celui	for-him, he, that-one, who-him

Word List (Old French to English)

Old French	English
cent	a-hundred, a-hundred
cerf	stag
ces	the
cest	this
c'est	it-is
ceval	horses
cha!	to-me
chaça	chased
chace	hunting
chacié	chased
chacier	hunt, the-hunt
chaï	fell
chaïr	fallen
chambre	chamber, chamber, room, royal apartment, territory
charga	loaded
chasvie	castle
cheïr	fell
chevalerie	chivalry, knights
chevaliers	gentleman, knight, knights
cheveleüre	hair
chi	here
chief	head, the-end
chien	dogs
chiens	dogs, hounds
chiere	dear, dearly-love
chierges	torches
chierté	affection, fondness
ci	here
ciel	heaven, the-skies
cil	he, him, that, the-one, they, this, this-he
cis	the, this
cité	city
clers	clear
cloie	enclosure
cloier	enclosure
coiement	secretly
col	neck, shoulders
colchié	laid-up
colchier	retire
comencha	began
commande	commanded
commandee	commended
comme	as, when
commença	began
commencement	stage
comment	how, how-to, just
compaigne	fields, troops
compaignie	company
con	as, recognised
c'on	where
coneü	made-known, recognised
coneüs	recognised
confondu	destroyed
confort	comfort
conqueroit	conquered
conquerre	capture, conquer
conrea	cultivated
conroi	care-of, retinue, the-trappings
conrois	retinue
conseü	pursued
conte	count, the-recounting
conté	recounted
conteça	contented
contee	recounted
contera	would-recount
conterent	heard
contre	against, compared with, to-greet, towards
contree	country, encountered
conut	recognised
corant	running
corent	steered
cors	body, heart
corsus	strong
cortois	courteous, courtly
cortoise	courtly
cortoisie	courtesy
corus	ran
cose	affair, creature, thing, things
costé	side
cosu	sewn
covrir	covered
cria	cried-out
crié	cried
croire	believe

Word List (Old French to English)

Old French	English
c'uns	one
cure	a-care, anxiety, care

D, d

Old French	English
damage	harm, harmed, trouble
dame	dame, lady, madam, woman
d'armes	arms, of-arms
d'artus	Arthur (a name)
de	by, from, of, out-of, than, the, to, with
deables	the-devil
deci	and-then, went
deduit	pleasure
degasté	laid-waste
del	from, of, of-the, of-this, to
delivrer	brought
demanda	asked, questions
demandast	asked-for
demande	asked, asked-for
demena	took
demené	of-took, took
demora	delayed
dermine	of-ermine
des	of, of-the, of-them
descaucha	removed-boots
descendu	dismounted.
deschaucier	remove-boots
desconfort	discomfort
descoplé	unleashed
deseure	only
desfaire	to-do
desira	desired
desnaturés	unnatural
despoille	clothes
despoillié	unclothed
despoilliés	unclothed
desroi	commotion
dessert	wasteland
destruioient	destroyed
detrancié	cut-up
deu	god, god's
devant	before, in front of, in the presence of, in-front
devenrai	I-shall-become
devenus	become
devint	became
devoit	was-to
di	day, say, tell
dïent	said, they-said, they-say
d'iluec	from-there
dirai	tell, will-tell
dirons	wel-tell
dis	says, tell
dist	said, saying, tell
dit	said
dites	tell
dobliers	plates
doi	finger, two
doignon	the-keep
dois	must, the-table
doit	finger, should
dolans	regret, sad, sorrow, unhappy
d'ome	of-a-man
d'ommes	of-men
dona	gave
done	gave
doné	gave
donrai	i-will-give
dons	gifts
dont	of which, of whom, of-where, of-whom, then, they-had, whose
dormir	to-sleep
dras	clothes
droit	direct, directly, proper, right, straight
drue	mistress
d'un	of-a
duré	endured
durement	greatly, hard, sorely, very
duveline	Dublin (a place)
dyrlande	of-Ireland
d'yrlande	from-Ireland, Ireland (a place), of-Ireland

Word List (Old French to English)

Old French	English

E, e

Old French	English
el	he, in, its, she, the
ele	he, she
en	and, at, go, he, in, into, is, of, of it, of-it, of-them, on, on top of, on-which, them, then, to, unto, was, with
enamé	he-loved
enbatus	entangled
enbracie	embraced
enbuissiés	embedded
encoloree	coloured
encor	still, yet
encore	still, yet
enfans	children
engané	tricked
engien	cheating, ingenuity, skill
engignié	tricked
engingnier	trick
enhaïrent	they-hated
enmena	taken-away
enmi	in-the-middle
enorgoillir	haughty
ens	in, inside, on
ensamble	together
ensi	so-as-this
entendés	listen
entra	entered
entr'aus	amongst
entré	entered
entrés	entered
envers	towards
environ	around, surrounded
erent	were
errant	were
erré	roamed
ert	to, was, who
es	in-those
esbanoier	enjoy
escapa	escape, escaped
escapé	escaped
escapés	escaped
escavie	charming
escilloit	ravaged
escouta	listen
escrié	shouted
escuier	squire
escuiers	squire
escus	shields
esgardés	look
eskiper	sail
espauleüre	shoulders
espees	swords
est	are, are, he, is, that, was, had, has, he, he-was, is, it-is, much, she, that, this, was
estant	standing
esté	be, been, had-been, was, were
estes	are
estoient	there-were, they-were
estoiles	stars
estoit	it-was, was, were
estraint	gripped
estrangla	strangled
estrier	stirrup
estris	strife
esturmans	steersman
et	and, him
eüs	of-them
eüsent	would-have
eüst	would-have
ex	eyes
explicit	now-is-the-end

F, f

Old French	English
face	to-do
faille	failed
faim	desire, hunger
faire	do, done, made, make, to-do, to-make
faisoient	they-were-making
faisoit	was-made

Word List (Old French to English)

Old French	English
fait	became, did, do, does, done, had, has-done, made, said, were
faites	doing, done, have, make, makes, word
faldra	fail
feme	wife, wife-his
femes	women
fera	will-make
ferés	do
ferés!	do
ferma	closed
feru	struck
fief	fief
fiex	son-of, sons
figure	character, form, person
fille	daughter
fin	end
fine	ends
firent	had, made
fist	be, been-so, had, has-it, was
flans	arms
foi	faith, honor
foi!'	faith
fois	times
font	they-did
forest	forest
forestier	foresters
formé	formed
forment	greatly, very, very much
fors	except, out, outside
forvoient	went
fu	became, came, had, happened, he, is, preparing, so, was
fuiant	running
fuissent	was-it-not-for
fuit	fled
furent	had, he-had, they-were, were
fus	were

G, g

Old French	English
gaitier	protect
gamais	sticks
gardés	guard
gardoient	kept
garnie	supplied
garnis	furnishing
gavain	Gawain (a name)
gavains	Gawain (a name)
gawain	Gawain's
gent	beautiful, fair, handsome, people, race
gente	elegant
gentil	brave, noble
gesir	lie, to-lie
geté	threw
giron	robe
gisant	lying
glorious	glorious
grans	great, large
grant	a-great, great, greatly, greay, large, tall, very
gravier	to-the-ground
gravoi	shore
guerre	trouble, war

H, h

Old French	English
haces	axes
haïst	hate-him
hasta	harried
hasté	haste
hastivement	quickly
haut	high
havene	harbour
hom	a-man, man
home	man, the-man
homes	men
honor	honour
honors	honour
honte	disgrace, shame, shamed

37

Word List (Old French to English)

Old French	English
hués	excited

I, i

Old French	English
i	a, an, he, i, is, one, she, there, they, with
ice	this
icel	one
ici	here
ii	two
iii	three
il	has, he, him, it, there, they
iluec	there
ira	at-once
iront	rode
issi	happened, here, so, thus
issiés	come
issirent	they-went
issu	went
issus	left
itel	the-same

J, j

Old French	English
ja	already, at once, at-once, ever, I, indeed, me, never, now
jadis	days-passed, in-days-passed
j'ai	I
jamais	never
je	I
jehiras	confess
jel	I, I-will
jesu	Jesus (a name)
jo	I, me, you
joians	joyed, joyful
joie	joy, rejoiced, rejoicing
jor	a-day, day
jors	day, days
joste	close, next-to
jut	lay

K, k

Old French	English
ke	which
kerra	believes
ki	him, of, that, which, who
kieutes	quilts
k'il	could-he, for-the, he-for, that, that-he, which-he

L, l

Old French	English
la	had, her, his, is, it, of, she-has, that, the, there, to-the
l'a	be, he, he-her, her, him, his, she, that, this
l'ai	have, of-him
lairai	shall-stop
lairés	let-be
lairomes	we-leave
lais	lay, lays, leave
laissa	he-left, left
laissast	let-be
laissier	abandon, leave, left, let, to-leave
laissons	let-us
lait	had, then
l'ait	has
l'ajornee	the-next-day
l'amerent	him-loved
lameront	him-they-would-love
lança	leaping
lande	heath, land
l'anel	the-ring
lardé	piece-of-meat, the-meat
lardoir	torn-to-pieces
largece	largesse
lart	the-article
las	lace
lassés	tired
l'assist	seated
l'aube	dawn

Word List (Old French to English)

Old French	English
l'autre	the-other
lava	washed
lavé	washed
l'aventure	the-adventure, the-event, the-story
l'avoient	had
l'avoit	had
l'avras	shall-have
le	he, her, he-was, him, his, it, one, she, the, they, this, who
l'en	he, he-him, her, here, him, him-there, of-them, there
l'endemain	the-morning
lenporta	it-took-away
les	by, he, her, his, let, the, them, they, this
l'escu	the-shield
lescuier	the-squire
l'escuier	the-squire
l'espaule	his-shoulder
lespousa	her-married
leu	a-wolf, wolf, wolves
leus	wolf, wolves
l'eüst	would-have
leva	rose, stood
levé	risen
levriers	greyhounds
li	as, but, he, her, he-was, him, his, it, of-them, she, the, they, this, to-him, was
l'i	her, him
lié	happy, joyful, pleased
lies	glad, happy
liés	glad, happy
lieu	place
lieues	leagues
lieus	places
liges	liege
lignage	family, lineage
lit	bed
l'iwain	Yvain's
loer	praised
l'oïrent	heard
longement	a-long-time, for a long time, long
l'ont	they, this-they, to-him-they
lor	from-them, his, their, them
l'orent	had
lors	he, then
losenga	persuaded
l'ostel	lodging, lodging
lot	heard
l'ot	before
lous	wolves
lués	As-soon-as
lui	he, he, him, her, him, king
l'uis	he-came-to, was
l'une	Of-one

M, m

Old French	English
m	a-thousand
ma	my
maçues	cudgels
main	hand, morning
maintenant	at-once, immediately, soon
mais	but, further, more, rather
maisnie	army, household
maison	dwelling, house
mal	bad, badly, disaster, evil, harm, ill, illness, mean, wretched
malbaillis	badly-done, in-trouble
malmenoient	attacked
malvaisement	evil
mandee	sent-for
mander	called-for, commanded
manel	my-hand
manga	ate
mangerai	i-will-eat
mangié	ate
mangier	eat, meal, the-meal
manoir	a-manor

Word List (Old French to English)

Old French	English
mantel	cloak, mantle
mar	in vain, wrong, wrongly
marine	sea
mariniers	mariners
maronier	mariners
m'atendés	wait-for-me
me	I, me, mine, to-me
meillor	better
Melïon	Melion (a name)
Melïon	Melion (a name)
Melïons	Melion (a name)
mellé	conflicts
memoire	memory
mena	taken, took
mené	he-took, took
menee	brought
mener	be-taken, lead, show, take, to-take
menés	taken, took
menoit	brought, many
menrés	take
mentirai	shall-lie
mer	pure, sea
merci	grace, mercy, pity
mercïé	thanked
merveille	intensely, marvel, marvellously, what is surprising, wonder, wonders
merveilles	marvels
merveillié	marvel
merveillier	amazement, marvel
mes	but, furthermore, he, me, message, more, my, with
m'est	is, mine-is
meterés	place
metra	life
meute	might
mi	him
mie	at-all, none-at-all, not, not-at-all
mis	set, treated
moi	me, mine, to-me
mollee	shaped
molt	many, much, very, very-much, very-well
mon	my
mont	mountain, world
monta	mounted, went-up
montaigne	mountain
montaignes	mountains
monte	mounted
monté	mounted
montee	mounted
montés	mounted
morir	death, die, kill
morras	die
mort	death, die, killed
mosterroie	I-will-show
mostra	showed
mot	word, words
mua	mutated
muciés	hidden

N, n

Old French	English
n'a	could-not, not-has, not-has-been, not-having
n'afubla	than-worn
n'ai	do-not-have
n'ait	is-not
namai	have-I-loved
n'ameroit	enamoured
n'autre	or-other
n'avoit	had-not, he-did-not-have, not-having
n'avrai	shall-I
ne	and not, can, could-not, he, naught, never, no, no-longer, none, no-one, nor, not, only, or, shall-not, you
nee	born
nef	ship, the-ship
nekedent	nevertheless
nel	among, did-not, none, nor, not, nothing
n'en	about, do-not, nor, not, not-of

Word List (Old French to English)

Old French	English
n'encontre	nor-meet
neporqant	even-though
nes	nose, noses, not
nestoie	I-shall-not-be
n'i	never, never-will, none, No-one, not
n'iert	another
nomer	call, called, name
non	don't, name, not, title
nu	naked
nues	bared
nuis	night
nuit	night
nul	any, anyone, no, none, not, not any
nus	naked, us, we

O, o

Old French	English
o	or, this, with
ocioient	killed
ocis	killed
ocit	killed
od	among, among, with, with
oï	heard, i-hear
oïr	hear
on	being, of, one, they
oncles	uncle
onques	ever, never, once
ont	they
or	gold, just, now
ore	hour, now, presently, soon, time
oré	wind
orent	had, had-they, heard, now, prayed, soon
osta	removed
oster	separate
ot	away, had, of, was, with
otroié	granted
otroier	agree, agree-to, grant
ou	or, this, where

P, p

Old French	English
pain	bread, piece-of-bread
paine	suffering, torment
pais	peace-treaty
païs	country, countryside, land, the-country, the-land
païsant	peasant
palais	palace, the-palace
palefroi	palfrey
par	by, by reason of, through
parage	family, origin, rank
parla	spoke, spoke-to, to-speak
parlé	spoken
parlement	conversation, meeting, word
parler	speak, speech, talk, to-talk-with
parleront	they-speak
pars	parts
part	part, portion
partir	leave, part-with, to-part
pas	not, passed
pasmee	fainting
passés	crossed
pechié	misfortune, mistake, sin
pendre	hang, hanged
pendus	hanging
pené	weary
penés	suffering
perdi	lost
perdu	lost
pere	father
pesa	troubled, weighed-upon
petite	petite
peüst	could, worse
piece	part, piece, segment, the-time, time
piere	prison, stone
pieres	stones
pies	feet, feet-of

41

Word List (Old French to English)

Old French	English	Old French	English
piés	fieet, the-feet	primes	first
pïés	feet	pris	esteem, prize, seized, took
pitié	pity	prist	pay, seized, took
place	place	priveement	privately
plaigne	plain	privés	tame
plain	full	proece	prowess
plenté	many, plenty	proié	begged
plora	wept	proisie	praised
plorant	weeping	prous	noble
plorer	cry, shed tears, weeping	pucele	girl, maiden, servant
plorés	i-implore-you	pucelë	maiden
plot	delighted	puceles	maidens
pluisors	many	puis	after, could, since, subsequently, then
plus	another, more, more-than, most	puisse	I-may
poés	may		
poi	but, few, little		
pooie	could		
pooit	could		

Q, q

Old French	English
qant	when
quanque	all that, what-he
quant	when
que	for, than, that, then, what, when, which, who
qu'ele	that-she, which-she
qu'en	that-in, which, will
querre	ask, asking-for, look for, to-seek, want
qu'est	what, which-is
qui	that, what, which, who
quide	believed
qu'il	that, what, which, which-of, which-that

Old French	English
por	because, for
porcoi	why
porent	could, could-they
porrai	could
porras	may
pors	boars
port	harbour, port, the-harbour, the-port
porté	brought, carried
portendus	stretched-out
portent	carried
porter	bring, brought, carried, carry, to-bear, wear
portoit	carried
pot	could
prandre	to-catch
premier	earli
prendra	would
prendrai	capture
prendre	seize, take, take hold of
prent	received, receives
pres	close
presentee	presented
pri	I-pray, pray

R, r

Old French	English
ravisa	noticed, recognised
ravisé	noticed
receüe	received
reconeüs	recognised
reconfort	recovery
reconforter	comfort
recorderent	repeated
redrecier	to-get-up

Word List (Old French to English)

Old French	English
regarda	glanced-at, looked-at
regarde	he-looked
regardé	looked, looked-at, looked-upon
regarder	look-at-him
regnoit	ruled
rehaiteroie	comfort
rehaitier	comfort
relevee	picked-up
remez	remained
remire	admired
reont	round
repairié	went
reposer	rest
reprendre	take-back
respont	responded
retenu	catch, retained
retorna	returned
retornee	returned
retornés	returned
rians	sparlking
riant	laughed
riche	expensive, generous, powerful, rich, splendid, strong
riches	rich, splendid
richoise	splendour
rien	any, anything, creature, nothing, person, thing
riviere	rivers
roi	kinf, king, kings, king's, the-king
roialme	the-kingdom
roiauté	realm
roïne	a-queen, queen
rois	king, king, nets, nets, the-king, the-nets
romains	Romans (a name)
rose	rose
rova	ordered
rové	begged

S, s

Old French	English
sa	for, had, her-own, his, how, this
sachierent	hoisted
sachiés	be-sure, knew, know, know-you
sacompaigna	accompanied
s'agenoilla	kneeling
sai	i-know
sailli	leapt
saisir	to-seize
sale	hall
salu	greet
salua	greeted
samblans	appearance
samblant	mannered
samit	rich-silk
sans	without
s'aresta	he-stopped
savoient	knew
savoit	knew
se	he, him, his, if, of, she, they, to
segnor	my-lords
sel	him
s'en	did-he, he, he-did, if, it, then, they, was, was-he, who
senescal	steward
sens	direction, sense
s'entrefirent	greeting
sera	there-will-be
serai	will-be
sergant	servants
seroie	become
seroit	was
seront	the-will-be
servi	served
servoient	served, they-served
ses	full, he, his, she, sight, the
sesjoï	rejoicing
s'est	he, he-is, he-was, is, was
set	knew, knowing, knows, seven
seul	alone, himself, only

Word List (Old French to English)

Old French	English	Old French	English
seule	alone, earthly life, world	tenir	consider, have, hold, keep, seize
seus	alone, single	tenoit	held
si	and, and moreover, and thus, as, but, him, his, if, so, such, that much, that way, then, this, thus, yet	tenu	beheld
		terre	country, earth, land
		terres	lands
		tertre	mound
		tes	your
s'i	they, thus	t'i	you
siecle	age, earthly life, world	tient	thought
siglant	sailing	tint	held, travelled, travels, went
s'il	if-he, if-him, whether		
sire	husband, my-lord, sire	ton	your
sisent	sat	torné	turned-to
socors	help	tornee	returned
soelent	only	tornerent	turned
soit	let-be	tornés	turned-away
son	her, his	tos	all
sont	are, made, they, was, went, were	tost	immediately, quickly, soon, soon-as
sor	above, on, over, to, upon	tostans	always, went, went-forwards
sos	under	tot	all, completely, entirely, every, was-all, whole
sot	found-out, knew		
sovent	frequently, many, often, time-to-time		
		tote	all
sui	am, i-am	totes	all
sus	above, up	toucerés	touch
sw	vow	toucha	touched
		touchast	touched-him

T, t

		toucherai	shall-touch
		touchié	touched
		touchier	to-touch
ta	your	touchiés	touch, touches
t'a	you-he	touciés	touched
tans	the-weather, time, weather	tous	all, completely
tant	as, as-much, so, so much, so-much, such, such-time, that, until	trace	trace
		traï	betrayed
		traïs	betrayed
tantost	immediately	traveillié	exhausted, suffered
tapis	carpets, hidden	traveilliés	tired
targa	delayed, waited	trente	thirty
targent	delayed	trestot	all
te	you	troeve	found
tel	had, has, much, such	trova	found
tendre	out-stretched	trovast	find

44

Word List (Old French to English)

Old French	English
trové	found
trovee	found
trovés	found
tu	you, you-will
tué	killed

U, u

Old French	English
u	or, where, whether
un	a, one
une	a, an, one
uns	one

V, v

Old French	English
va	went
vaches	cows
vairs	bright
vait	goes, went
vallet	servant
veés	look, see
veïr	see
veïsciés	would-have-seen
veneor	huntsmen
vengié	avenged
venir	come, coming, go
venoit	came, went
venra	would-go
vens	the-wind
vent	wind
venu	came, went
venue	arrival, arrived, arriving
venus	came, come, veering
verde	green
verité	the-truth, true
vermeil	vermillion
vermeille	crimson
verra	watch
vers	against, to, toward, towards, went
ves	se
vesti	dressed
vestu	wearing
veu	vows, wishes
veü	known-him, saw, seen, watched
veüe	saw
veus	want
veüs	saw
vie	life, live
vienent	came, they-came
vin	wine
vindrent	saw, they-went
vint	came, went
virent	saw, they-saw
vis	face, knew, so
vit	saw, seen
vo	your
voa	vow
voi!	I-see
voient	they-saw
voiles	sails
voille	wishing
voir	indeed, true, truly, truth
voit	saw
volenté	he-wished, wish
volentés	wished
volentiers	gladly, he-wanted, willing, willingly
voloie	wish, wished
voloit	he-wanted-to, he-wished, wished, wished-to
volt	wanted, wants, willed, wished
vont	went
vos	to-you, you, your
vostre	your
vout	wanted, wished
vrais	true

W, w

X, x

Old French	English
x	ten

Word List (Old French to English)

Old French   English

xi   eleven
xv   fifteen
xx   twenty

Y, y

Ydel   Ydel (a name)
Yrïen   Yrien (a name)
Yrlande   Ireland (a place)

Z, z

Word List *(English to Old French)*

English	Old French

0-9

A, a

English	Old French
a	a, i, un, une
above	sor
a-care	cure
accompanied	sacompaigna
a-day	jor
addressed	apela
admired	remire
adventure	aventure
affection	chierté
age	siecle
aggressively	angoissant
a-great	grant
agreement	acorder
agree-to	otroier
a-hundred	c, cent
all	tos, tot, tote, totes, tous, trestot
alone	seul, seule, seus
along	ala
a-long-time	longement
already	ja
always	tostans
am	sui
a-man	hom
a-manor	manoir
amazement	merveillier
among	od
among, with	od
amongst	entr'aus
an	i, une
and	a, en, et, si
and-then	deci
animals	almaille
another	n'iert, plus
any	nul
appearance	samblans
appeared	aparut
approach	adesés
approached	adesé
a-queen	roïne
are	estes, sont
are, he, is, that, was	est
arms	d'armes, flans
around	a, environ
arrived	arivé, arivés, venue
arriving	venue
Arthur	artu, artus, d'artus
Arthur (a name)	Artus
as	a, comme, con, li, si
asked	demanda
asked-for	demandast, demande
as-much	tant
As-soon-as	lués
as-this	c'ainc
at	a, al, as, en
at-all	mie
ate	manga, mangié
a-thousand	m
at-once	ira, ja, maintenant
attacked	abatu, malmenoient
attended	atendu
at-the	as
at-this-point	aïtant
avenged	vengié
away	ot
a-wolf	leu
axes	haces

Æ, æ

B, b

English	Old French
badly-done	malbaillis
bared	nues
baron	baron
barons	baron, barons

Word List (English to Old French)

English	*Old French*	English	*Old French*
basin	*bacin*	came	*fu, venoit, venu, venus, vienent, vint*
be	*fist, l'a*		
beasts	*bestes*	capture	*prendrai*
beautiful	*beaus, beax, bel, bele, gent*	care	*cure*
		care-of	*conroi*
beauty	*bele*	carpets	*tapis*
became	*devint, fait, fu*	carried	*aporté, porté, portent, porter, portoit*
because	*car, por*		
become	*devenus, seroie*	casting	*caston*
bed	*lit*	castle	*castel, chasvie*
before	*devant, l'ot*	catch	*retenu*
began	*comencha, commença*	chamber	*cambre, chambre*
		chamberlain	*canberlenc*
begged	*proié, rové*	chamberlains	*canberlens*
beheld	*tenu*	chambers	*canbres*
being	*on*	charming	*escavie*
believe	*croire*	chased	*chaça, chacié*
believed	*quide*	children	*enfans*
believes	*kerra*	chivalry	*chevalerie*
beloved	*bel*	city	*cité*
be-sure	*sachiés*	clear	*clers*
betrayed	*traï, traïs*	cloak	*mantel*
better	*meillor*	close	*joste, pres*
blonde	*blonde*	closed	*ferma*
boars	*pors*	clothes	*despoille, dras*
body	*cors*	coloured	*encoloree*
born	*nee*	come	*issiés, venus*
both	*andeus*	comfort	*confort, reconforter, rehaiteroie, rehaitier*
bright	*vairs*		
brought	*amenee, aporter, aporterent, delivrer, menee, menoit, porté*	coming	*venir*
		commanded	*commande, mander*
		commended	*commandee*
brought-down	*abatu*	commotion	*desroi*
burdened	*bailli*	company	*compaignie*
burned	*ardoir*	completely	*tot, tous*
bush	*buisson*	confess	*jehiras*
but	*li, mais*	conflicts	*mellé*
by	*a, les, par*	conquer	*conquerre*
		conquered	*conqueroit*
		contented	*conteça*
		could	*peüst, pooie, pooit, porent, porrai, pot*

C, c

English	*Old French*	English	*Old French*
cajoled	*blandi*	could-he	*k'il*
called	*apela, apelé, apelés, araisniés, nomer*	could-not	*n'a, ne*
		country	*contree, païs, terre*
called-for	*mander*	countryside	*païs*

Word List (English to Old French)

English	Old French
courteous	cortois
courtesy	cortoisie
courtly	cortois, cortoise
covered	covrir
cows	vaches
cried	crié
cried-out	cria
crimson	vermeille
crossed	passés
cudgels	maçues
cultivated	conrea
cut-up	detrancié

D, d

English	Old French
dark	avespré
daughter	fille
dawn	l'aube
day	jor, jors
days	jors
dear	chiere
dearly-love	chiere
death	morir, mort
delayed	demora, targa, targent
delaying	atarga
delighted	plot
desired	desira
destroyed	confondu, destruioient
did	fait
did-not	nel
die	morras, mort
directly	droit
discomfort	desconfort
dismounted.	descendu
do	fait, ferés, ferés!
does	fait
dogs	chien
doing	faites
do-not-have	n'ai
don't	non
downcast	asopli
drank	beü, beüt
dressed	vesti
Dublin	duveline
dwelling	maison

E, e

English	Old French
each	cascuns
earli	premier
eat	mangier
elegant	bele, gente
eleven	xi
embedded	enbuissiés
embraced	baisié, enbracie
enamoured	n'ameroit
enclosure	cloie, cloier
encountered	contree
end	fin
ends	fine
endured	duré
enemies	anemis
enjoy	esbanoier
entangled	enbatus
entered	entra, entré, entrés
equipped	apareillie
escape	escapa
escaped	escapa, escapé, escapés
esteem	pris
evening-fell	avespra
even-though	neporqant
evil	malvaisement
excellence	bonté
except	fors
excited	hués
exhausted	traveillié
eyes	ex

F, f

English	Old French
face	vis
fail	faldra
failed	faille
fainting	pasmee
fair	bon
fair-lady	bele
faith	foi, foi!'
fallen	chaïr

Word List (English to Old French)

English	*Old French*	English	*Old French*
family	*parage*	going	*alé, alés*
father	*pere*	gone	*alé, alés*
feet	*pies, pïés*	good	*biaus, bon, bone, bons*
feet	*piés*		
feet-of	*pies*	granted	*otroié*
fell	*chaï, cheïr*	great	*grans, grant*
fief	*fief*	greatly	*durement, forment, grant*
fields	*compaigne*		
fifteen	*xv*	greay	*grant*
find	*trovast*	green	*verde*
finger	*doit*	greet	*salu*
first	*primes*	greeted	*salua*
fled	*fuit*	greeting	*s'entrefirent*
for	*car, por, que*	greyhounds	*levriers*
forest	*bois, forest*	gripped	*estraint*
foresters	*forestier*	guard	*gardés*
forests	*bois*		
formed	*formé*		
for-the	*k'il*		
forward	*avant*		

H, h

English	*Old French*
found	*troeve, trova, trové, trovee, trovés*
found-out	*sot*
frequently	*sovent*
from	*de, del*
from-Ireland	*d'yrlande*
from-them	*lor*
from-there	*d'iluec*
full	*plain*
furnishing	*garnis*
further	*avant*

English	*Old French*
had	*a, avoit, est, fait, firent, fist, fu, furent, lait, l'avoient, l'avoit, l'orent, orent, ot, sa*
had-been	*esté*
had-he	*a*
had-not	*n'avoit*
had-they	*orent*
hair	*cheveleüre*
hall	*sale*
hand	*main*
hanged	*pendre*
hanging	*pendus*
happened	*avenu, fu*
happy	*lies, liés*
harbour	*havene, port*
hard	*durement*
harm	*mal*
harmed	*damage*
harried	*hasta*
has	*a, avra, est, il, l'ait*
haste	*hasté*
hate-him	*haïst*
haughty	*enorgoillir*
have	*ai, as, auroit, avés, avoir, faites, l'ai*
have-I	*ai*

G, g

English	*Old French*
gave	*dona, done, doné*
Gawain	*gavain, gavains*
Gawain's	*gawain*
gifts	*dons*
glad	*lies, liés*
gladly	*volentiers*
glanced-at	*regarda*
glorious	*glorious*
go	*ala, aler, alés*
god	*deu*
god's	*deu*

50

Word List (English to Old French)

English	*Old French*
have-I-loved	*namai*
he	*a, ce, celui, cil, el, en, est, fu, i, il, l'a, le, l'en, les, li, lors, lui, ne, se, s'en, ses, s'est*
he, him	*lui*
head	*chief*
hear	*oïr*
heard	*antendu, conterent, l'oïrent, lot, oï, orent*
heath	*lande*
he-came-to	*l'uis*
he-did	*s'en*
he-did-not-have	*n'avoit*
he-for	*k'il*
he-had	*avoit*
he-her	*l'a*
he-him	*l'en*
he-is	*s'est*
held	*tenoit, tint*
he-left	*laissa*
he-looked	*regarde*
he-loved	*ama, enamé*
help	*socors*
her	*la, l'a, le, les, li, l'i, lui, son*
here	*chi, ci, ici, l'en*
her-married	*lespousa*
her-own	*sa*
he-stopped	*s'aresta*
he-took	*mené*
he-wanted-to	*voloit*
he-was	*est, le, li, s'est*
he-went	*ala*
he-wished	*volenté, voloit*
hidden	*celé, muciés, tapis*
hide	*celes*
high	*haut*
him	*et, il, l'a, le, l'en, li, lui, mi, se, sel, si*
him-loved	*l'amerent*
himself	*seul*
him-there	*l'en*
him-they-would-love	*lameront*
his	*la, l'a, le, les, li, lor, sa, se, ses, si, son*
his-shoulder	*l'espaule*
hoisted	*sachierent*
hold	*tenir*
honour	*honor, honors*
horses	*ceval*
hounds	*chiens*
household	*maisnie*
how	*comment, sa*
how-to	*comment*
hunger	*faim*
hunt	*chacier*
hunting	*chace*
huntsmen	*veneor*

I, i

English	*Old French*
I	*ja, j'ai, je, jel, jo*
I-am	*sui*
if	*se, si*
if-he	*s'il*
i-implore-you	*plorés*
I-know	*sai*
ill	*mal*
illuminated	*alumer*
I-may	*puisse*
immediately	*tantost, tost*
in	*al, as, el, en, ens*
in-accord	*acorda*
in-choice	*anchois*
in-days-passed	*jadis*
indeed	*ja*
in-front	*devant*
ingenuity	*engien*
inside	*ens*
intensely	*merveille*
in-the-middle	*enmi*
in-those	*es*
into	*en*
in-trouble	*malbaillis*
I-pray	*pri*
Ireland	*d'yrlande*
Ireland (a place)	*Yrlande*
is	*as, est, s'est*
I-see	*voi!*
I-shall-become	*devenrai*
I-shall-bring	*aporterai*

Word List (English to Old French)

English	Old French	English	Old French
I-shall-not-be	*nestoie*	laid-up	*colchié*
is-not	*n'ait*	laid-waste	*degasté*
it	*a, il, le, li*	land	*lande, païs, terre*
it-is	*c'est, est*	lands	*terres*
its	*el*	large	*grans, grant*
it-took-away	*lenporta*	largesse	*largece*
it-was	*estoit*	laughed	*riant*
I-will	*jel*	lay	*jut, lais*
i-will-eat	*mangerai*	leagues	*lieues*
i-will-give	*donrai*	leaping	*lança*
I-will-show	*mosterroie*	leapt	*sailli*
		leave	*lais, partir*
		left	*issus, laissa*
		let-be	*lairés, laissast, soit*
		let-us	*laissons*

J, j

English	Old French
Jesus	*jesu*
joy	*joie*
joyed	*joians*
joyful	*joians*
just	*comment*

English	Old French
lie	*gesir*
liege	*liges*
life	*metra, vie*
lineage	*lignage*
listen	*entendés, escouta*
little	*poi*
live	*vie*
loaded	*charga*
lodging	*l'ostel*
look	*esgardés, veés*
look-at-him	*regarder*
looked	*regardé*
looked-at	*regarda, regardé*
looked-upon	*regardé*
lost	*perdi, perdu*
love	*amor*
loved	*amé, amee, amer*
lowered	*baissié*
lying	*gisant*

K, k

English	Old French
kept	*gardoient*
killed	*mort, ocioient, ocis, ocit, tué*
kinf	*roi*
king	*lui, roi, rois*
kings	*roi*
king's	*roi*
kissed	*baisa, baisie*
kneeling	*s'agenoilla*
knew	*sachiés, savoient, savoit, set, sot, vis*
knight	*bacheler*
knights	*chevalerie, chevaliers*
know	*sachiés*
knowing	*set*
know-you	*sachiés*

M, m

English	Old French
made	*fait, firent, sont*
made-known	*coneü*
maiden	*pucele, pucelë*
maidens	*puceles*
man	*hom, home*
mannered	*samblant*
mantle	*mantel*

L, l

English	Old French
lace	*las*
lady	*dame*

Word List (English to Old French)

English	*Old French*	English	*Old French*
many	*menoit, molt, plenté, pluisors*	next-to	*joste*
mariners	*mariniers, maronier*	night	*nuis, nuit*
marvel	*merveille, merveillié, merveillier*	night-fall	*anuita*
		noble	*gentil, prous*
marvels	*merveilles*	no-longer	*ne*
may	*poés, porras*	none	*ne, nel, nul*
me	*ja, me, moi*	none-at-all	*mie*
meal	*mangier*	no-one	*ne*
meeting	*parlement*	nor	*ne, nel*
Melion (a name)	*Melïon, Melïon., Melïons*	nor-meet	*n'encontre*
		not	*ne, nel, n'en, n'en, nes, n'i, nul, pas*
memory	*memoire*	not-at-all	*mie*
men	*homes*	not-has-been	*n'a*
mercy	*merci*	not-having	*n'a, n'avoit*
message	*mes*	nothing	*nel, rien*
might	*meute*	noticed	*ravisa, ravisé*
mine	*me, moi*	not-of	*n'en*
mine-is	*m'est*	now	*adont, or, ore, orent*
misfortune	*pechié*	now-is-the-end	*explicit*
mistress	*drue*		
more	*mais, plus*		
more-than	*plus*		
morning	*main*		
most	*plus*		
mound	*tertre*		
mountain	*montaigne*		
mountains	*montaignes*		
mounted	*monta, monte, monté, montee, montés*		
mouth	*bouche*		
much	*est, molt*		
must	*dois*		
mutated	*mua*		
my	*ma, mon*		
my-hand	*manel*		
my-lords	*segnor*		

O, o

English	*Old French*
oars	*aviron*
of	*a, al, de, del, des, en, on, se*
of-a	*d'un*
of-a-man	*d'ome*
of-arms	*d'armes*
of-ermine	*dermine*
off	*a*
of-Ireland	*dyrlande, d'yrlande*
of-it	*en*
of-men	*d'ommes*
Of-one	*l'une*
of-the	*del, des*
of-them	*des, en, eüs, l'en, li*
of-took	*demené*
of-where	*dont*
of-whom	*dont*
on	*a, en, ens, sor*
one	*c'uns, i, icel, on, un, une, uns*
only	*deseure, ne, seul, soelent*

N, n

English	*Old French*
naked	*nu, nus*
neck	*col*
nets	*rois*
never	*ja, jamais, ne, n'i, onques*
nevertheless	*nekedent*

Word List (English to Old French)

English	Old French	English	Old French
on-which	en	proceed	aler
or	ne, ou, u	protect	gaitier
ordered	rova	prowess	proece
or-other	n'autre	pursued	conseü
other	altre, autre		
out	fors		
outside	fors		
out-stretched	tendre		
over	sor		
oxen	bues		

Q, q

English	Old French
queen	roïne
quickly	hastivement, tost
quilts	kieutes
quiver	bercerië

P, p

English	Old French
palace	palais
palfrey	palefroi
part	part
parts	pars
passed	pas
peace-treaty	pais
peasant	païsant
people	gent
person	figure
persuaded	losenga
petite	petite
picked-up	relevee
piece-of-bread	pain
piece-of-meat	lardé
pity	pitié
place	lieu, meterés, place
places	lieus
plain	plaigne
plates	dobliers
pleased	bel, lié
pleasure	deduit
plenty	plenté
politely	belement
port	port
praised	loer, proisie
pray	pri
prayed	orent
prepare	atornés
prepared	apareillié, apareillier
preparing	fu
presented	presentee
privately	priveement

R, r

English	Old French
ran	corus
rather	ainc, ains, assez
ravaged	escilloit
ready	apresté
realm	roiauté
received	prent, receüe
recognised	con, coneü, coneüs, conut, ravisa, reconeüs
recounted	aconté, conté, contee
recovery	reconfort
regret	dolans
rejoiced	joie
rejoicing	joie, sesjoï
remained	remez
remove-boots	deschaucier
removed	osta
removed-boots	descaucha
repeated	recorderent
responded	respont
rest	reposer
retinue	conroi, conrois
retire	colchier
returned	atorna, retorna, retornee, retornés, tornee
rich	riche, riches
rich-silk	samit
right	droit
ring	anel

Word List (English to Old French)

English	*Old French*	English	*Old French*
risen	*levé*	shall-lie	*mentirai*
risked	*aventure*	shall-not	*ne*
rivers	*riviere*	shall-stop	*lairai*
roamed	*erré*	shall-touch	*toucherai*
robe	*giron*	shamed	*honte*
rode	*iront*	shaped	*mollee*
Romans	*romains*	she	*ele, est, i, l'a, le, se, ses*
rose	*leva, rose*		
round	*reont*	she-has	*la*
ruined	*agastis*	shields	*escus*
ruled	*regnoit*	ship	*nef*
running	*corant, fuiant*	shore	*gravoi*
		shortly	*briement*
		should	*doit*
		shoulders	*col, espauleüre*
		shouted	*escrié*

S, s

English	*Old French*	English	*Old French*
sad	*dolans*	showed	*mostra*
said	*dïent, dist, dit, fait*	side	*costé*
sail	*eskiper*	single	*seus*
sailing	*siglant*	sire	*sire*
sails	*voiles*	so	*ce, si*
sat	*sisent*	so-as-this	*ensi*
saw	*veü, veüe, veüs, vindrent, virent, vit, voit*	some	*alqant*
		somewhat	*alques*
		so-much	*tant*
say	*di*	son-of	*fiex*
saying	*dist*	sons	*fiex*
says	*dis*	soon	*ore, orent*
se	*ves*	soon-as	*tost*
sea	*marine, mer*	sorely	*durement*
seated	*assis, l'assist*	sorrow	*dolans*
secretly	*coiement*	sparlking	*rians*
see	*veés, veïr*	speak	*parler*
seen	*vit*	speech	*parler*
seized	*pris, prist*	splendid	*riche, riches*
sense	*sens*	splendour	*richoise*
sent-for	*mandee*	spoke	*parla*
separate	*oster*	spoken	*parlé*
servant	*vallet*	spoke-to	*parla*
servants	*sergant*	squire	*escuier, escuiers*
served	*servi, servoient*	stag	*cerf*
set	*mis*	stage	*commencement*
sewn	*cosu*	standing	*estant*
shall-have	*l'avras*	stars	*estoiles*
shall-I	*n'avrai*	steered	*corent*
shall-I-love	*amerai*	steersman	*esturmans*

Word List (English to Old French)

English	Old French	English	Old French
steward	senescal	the-article	lart
stick	baston	the-country	païs
sticks	gamais	the-devil	deables
still	encor, encore	the-feet	piés
stirrup	estrier	the-forest	bois
stone	piere	the-harbour	port
stones	pieres	the-hunt	chacier
stood	leva	their	lor
stopped	arestus	the-keep	doignon
stopping	arestés	the-king	roi, rois
straight	droit	the-kingdom	roialme
strangled	estrangla	the-land	païs
stretched-out	portendus	them	en, les, lor
strife	estris	the-man	home
strong	corsus	the-meal	mangier
struck	feru	the-meat	lardé
such	si, tel	the-morning	l'endemain
suffered	traveillié	then	a, dont, en, lait, lors, puis, que, s'en, si
suffering	paine, penés	the-nets	rois
supplied	garnie	the-next-day	l'ajornee
surrounded	avironé, environ	the-other	l'autre
swords	espees	the-port	port
		there	i, il, iluec, la
		the-recounting	conte
		there-were	estoient

T, t

English	Old French	English	Old French
		there-will-be	sera
take	menrés, prendre	the-ring	l'anel
take-back	reprendre	the-same	itel
taken	mena, menés	the-shield	l'escu
taken-away	enmena	the-ship	nef
tame	privés	the-skies	ciel
tell	dirai, dites	the-squire	lescuier, l'escuier
ten	x	the-table	dois
than	de	the-trappings	conroi
thanked	mercïé	the-truth	verité
than-worn	n'afubla	the-weather	tans
that	a, ce, cel, cil, k'il, la, que	the-will-be	seront
		the-wind	vens
that-Arthur	c'artus	the-woods	boscage
that-he	k'il	they	cil, i, il, le, les, li, l'ont, on, ont, se, s'en, s'i, sont
that-in	qu'en		
that-she	qu'ele		
the	a, as, cel, cele, ces, cis, de, el, la, le, les, li, ses	they-came	vienent
		they-did	font
the-adventure	l'aventure	they-had	avoient, dont

56

Word List (English to Old French)

English	Old French	English	Old French
they-hated	enhaïrent	to-seize	saisir
they-said	dïent	to-sleep	dormir
they-saw	virent, voient	to-speak	parla
they-say	dïent	to-take	mener
they-served	servoient	to-the	al, ax
they-speak	parleront	to-the-ground	gravier
they-went	issirent, vindrent	to-touch	touchier
they-were	estoient, furent	touch	toucerés, touchiés
they-were-making	faisoient	touched	toucha, touchié, touciés
things	cose	touched-him	touchast
thirty	trente	touches	touchiés
this	a, ce, cel, cele, cest, cil, cis, est, ice, l'a, le, les, li, sa, si	towards	contre, envers, vers
		to-you	vos
this-they	l'ont	trace	trace
Those	celes	trick	engingnier
thought	tient	tricked	engané, engignié
three	iii	troubled	pesa
threw	geté	true	
thus	adont, ça, issi, si	true	
time	piece, tans	truly	voir
times	fois	truth	voir
tired	lassés, traveilliés	turned	tornerent
to	a, al, en, ert, sor, vers	turned-away	tornés
to-bear	porter	turned-to	torné
to-bring	anemis	twenty	xx
to-catch	prandre	two	doi, ii
to-do	desfaire, face, faire		
together	ensamble		
to-get-up	redrecier		
to-go	aler		

U, u

English	Old French
to-greet	contre
to-him	li
to-him-they	l'ont
to-leave	laissier
to-lie	gesir
to-love	amer
to-make	faire
to-me	cha!, moi
tonight	anuit
took	demena, demené, mena, mené, menés, pris, prist
torches	chierges
torn-to-pieces	lardoir
to-seek	querre

English	Old French
uncle	oncles
unclothed	despoillié, despoilliés
under	sos
unhappy	dolans
unleashed	descoplé
unnatural	desnaturés
until	tant
up	amont, sus
upon	sor

V, v

English	Old French
veering	venus
vermillion	vermeil

Word List (English to Old French)

English	*Old French*	English	*Old French*
very	*durement, grant, molt*	what	*que, qu'est*
very-much	*molt*	what-he	*quanque*
very-well	*assés, molt*	when	*qant, quant, que*
vow	*sw, voa*	where	*c'on, ou, u*
vows	*veu*	which	*ke, ki, que, qu'en, qui, qu'il*

W, w

		which-he	*k'il*
		which-is	*qu'est*
		which-she	*qu'ele*
wait	*atendu*	white	*blance*
waited	*atendi, targa*	who	*ert, ki, que, qui*
wait-for-me	*m'atendés*	why	*porcoi*
waiting	*atendi*	wife	*feme*
want	*veus*	wife-his	*feme*
wanted	*volt, vout*	will	*qu'en*
war	*guerre*	will-be	*serai*
was	*a, avoit, en, ert, est, estoit, fist, fu, l'uis, ot, s'en, seroit, s'est, sont*	willed	*volt*
		will-he-have	*avra*
		willingly	*volentiers*
was-all	*tot*	will-make	*fera*
was-he	*s'en*	wind	*oré, vent*
washed	*lava, lavé*	wine	*vin*
was-it-not-for	*fuissent*	wish	*volenté, voloie*
was-made	*faisoit*	wished	*volentés, voloie, voloit, volt, vout*
wasteland	*dessert*		
was-to	*devoit*	wished-to	*voloit*
watch	*verra*	wishes	*veu*
watched	*veü*	wishing	*voille*
wearing	*vestu*	with	*a, avoec, en, i, o, od, ot*
weary	*pené*		
weeping	*plorant, plorer*	without	*sans*
weighed-upon	*pesa*	wolf	*leu, leus*
we-leave	*lairomes*	wolves	*leu, leus, lous*
well	*assés, bel, bien*	women	*femes*
wel-tell	*dirons*	wood	*bois*
went	*alé, alés, deci, forvoient, issu, repairié, sont, tint, tostans, va, vait, venoit, venu, vint, vont*	woods	*bois*
		word	*faites*
		words	*mot*
		world	*mont*
		would	*prendra*
went-forwards	*tostans*	would-go	*venra*
went-to	*alés*	would-have	*eüsent, eüst, l'eüst*
went-up	*monta*	would-have-seen	*veïsciés*
wept	*plora*	would-recount	*contera*
were	*erent, errant, esté, estoit, fait, furent, fus, sont*	wrapped	*afublez*
		wrong	*mar*

Word List (English to Old French)

English	Old French
wrongly	*mar*

X, x

Y, y

Ydel (a name)	*Ydel*
year	*an*
years	*ans*
you	*as, jo, te, t'i, tu, vos*
you-he	*t'a*
your	*ta, tes, ton, vo, vos, vostre*
you-will	*tu*
Yrien (a name)	*Yrïen*
Yvain's	*l'iwain*

Z, z

www.ingramcontent.com/pod-product-compliance
Lightning Source LLC
Chambersburg PA
CBHW051424070526
44584CB00023B/3565